Marquart's Works

VOLUME
VI

JUSTIFICATION

Edited by
Herman J. Otten

LUTHERAN NEWS, INC., New Haven, Missouri

TABLE OF CONTENTS

FOREWORD

Dr. Marquart was a beloved Professor by all the students that sat in his classes. His ability to simplify great theological concepts made him a favorite Teacher for all the students who attended the Seminary. He not only instilled in us a love for Theology, but he also showed us how it was to be applied in a pastor's daily calling.

However, these writings are not just for pastors. Even dedicated laymen will be able to grasp and learn from this great Teacher of the Church. Whenever and wherever Dr. Marquart made a presentation, you would soon see that he was eagerly sought out, not just by pastors but also by laymen. They too recognized his genius in refuting those who denied the Word of God. He was as popular with laymen as he was with pastors. Here in these volumes you will once again be able to take your place and listen to this great Teacher, as he clearly enunciates various topics from a thoroughly Lutheran perspective. Since these multiple volumes consist of the various topics that Dr. Marquart addressed over his illustrious life, you will find it hard to put these volumes down.

Having Dr. Marquart's writings in book form will once again allow this fearless Champion of the Church to speak to the issues that continue to plague the Church from one generation to the next. False doctrine continues to be rehashed and sent out with new clothes. As the Proverb goes, "there is nothing new under the sun." Dr. Marquart had the remarkable ability to dissect what the issue was, and why it was, and still is, false doctrine. Confessional Lutherans from all over the world were always eager to attend Dr. Marquart's lectures. They recognized that he was a giant among men. Anyone concerned about the welfare of the Church will want to have these volumes on their bookshelf.

It appears that the Almighty Savior of the Church, in His infinite wisdom, chooses to send out only a few Teachers of the Church. One may make a very short list of these esteemed gifts from God. Luther, Chemnitz, Gerhard, Walther, Pieper, Preus, and Marquart. Their writings stand the test of time. These men did not write for some passing fad, that is here today and then blown away by tomorrow's changing wind vane. Any pastor or layman, who has a desire and love for the Truth, will not be disappointed with these volumes. Every congregation that has a love for the Lord and His saving Gospel, would do well to purchase the writings from these Teachers of the Church. God had His good reasons for raising these men up and sending them out, and it would be wise for pastors and laymen to read, mark, learn and inwardly digest the writings of these great defenders of the Gospel.

Rev. Herman Otten is to be commended for publishing the writings of Dr. Kurt Marquart. This may well be Rev. Otten's finest and most enduring contribution to the Church.

Rev. Ray R. Ohlendorf
Salem Lutheran Church
Taylorsville, NC
4th Sunday in Lent 2014

Acknowledgements

Well Herman,

As usual you find yourself doing what unsere beliebte Synode should have done long ago. The fact that CPH has not already published a book of Kurt's writings is an absolute travesty. It is an indictment of the politics before theology which has destroyed the orthodoxy of the LCMS. Our Savior Lutheran Church will stand by you in the worthy project. Back in the dark days when Bohlmann and his supporters were after Robert Preus we published a number of Kurt's magnificent essays on Robert's behalf. Modern Missouri has never produced another theologian comparable to him either in confessional fidelity or eloquence. We are proud and eager to take part in this belated effort. "Gottes Wort Und Luthers Lehr Vergehet Nun Und Nimmermehr."

Larry White, Pastor
Our Saviour Lutheran Church
Houston, Texas

Thanks to Luke Otten for arranging the publication of these volumes and to Naomi Finck for type-setting.

Thanks to Grace Otten for recognizing the importance of publishing *Marquart's Works* ever since they first began appearing in *Christian News* more than 50 years ago. Thanks to Scott Meyer, "America's confessional Lutheran" lay historian and President of the Concordia Historical Institute whose appreciation of Marquart's works and encouragement helped make the publication of these volumes possible.

PREFACE

Dr. C. F. W. Walther, first president of The Lutheran Church-Missouri Synod, has been rightly referred to as "The American Luther." As the editor of a Christian weekly for 51 years, the undersigned has reviewed thousands of books. During all these years he has published the writings of many theologians. The index at the back of Volume V of the *Christian News Encyclopedia* lists the names of hundreds of theologians whose writings have appeared in *Christian News*. Some, like Kurt Marquart, were also good friends. Yet, the editor knows of no theologian who deserves the title "The International Lutheran" more than Kurt Marquart. The editor's wife, Grace, is a graduate of Concordia College, St. Paul Minnesota and Valparaiso University. There she studied under some prominent theologians who later became professors at Concordia Seminary, St. Louis and Seminex. In 1963 Grace Otten and Kurt Marquart were *CN*'s reporters at the Fourth Assembly of the Lutheran World Federation in Helsinki, Finland. Following the LWF Assembly she and the editor's brother, Walter, who knew Marquart for 54 years, accompanied him on a twenty city lecture tour in the U.S. Grace shares the editor's evaluation of Kurt Marquart. She helped make it possible together with Luke Otten, Ruth Rethemeyer, Mary Beth Otten, Kristina Bailey and the Missourian Publishing Company, Washington, Missouri, to get *Marquart's Legacy* published in 2006 not long after his death. The 76 page *Marquart's Legacy* is available from *Christian News* for $5.00. It includes photos of Marquart and family and information about two professionally made videos showing Marquart in action.

Marquart's Legacy begins with a brief biography of Kurt Marquart. Then follows "Remembrances of a Former Seminary Roommate," the editor of *Christian News*. Next comes "The Lasting Legacy of Kurt Marquart" as expressed by many who knew him well.

The appendixes list the writings and reports of Kurt Marquart which have appeared in 44 volumes of *Christian News* (1962-2006), *A Christian Handbook on Vital Issues*, the five volumes of the *Christian News Encyclopedia, Luther Today, What Would He Do or Say?* and *Crisis in Christendom-Seminex Ablaze*. The lasting legacy of a great theologian and genius like Kurt Marquart can best be found in his works. *CN* suggested in 2006 that the Lutheran Church-Missouri Synod's Concordia Publishing House should publish *Marquart's Works*.

The questions at the end of each section are included to make *Marquart's Works* helpful for study. In an age when faith in historic Christianity is declining in all of the major denominations, *Marquart's Works* can be used to encourage and strengthen faithful Christians and begin a 21st Century Reformation and 21st Century *Formula of Concord* by the 500th anniversary of the Reformation in 2017.

Herman Otten
Reformation, 2014

iii

LET'S ASK SCRIPTURE AND TRADITION ABOUT SCRIPTURE AND TRADITION

WHY THIS TREATISE?

When Lutherans and Roman Catholics fall in love they are often blissfully unaware-except in a vague or even distorted way—of the real differences between the two churches. And love is blind. That has its good points of course. But in matters of faith, romance dare not lure vision and judgment. It is in this interest that this little treatise has been compiled. It deals factually and logically with ONE important difference between the two churches. While these few pages cannot of course say everything on the subject, they do give a concise overview of the basic issues, which must be kept in clear focus if the discussion is to be relevant. The essay is offered in Christian friendship to those concerned, in the hope that it will lead to further and deeper personal study on the part of those who love the truth.

I. THE DIFFERENCE

The Voice of Rome:

"The most sacred Synod of Trent, recognizing that this truth and discipline are contained in the written books **and the unwritten traditions** . . . accepts and venerates, with **equally devout affection and reverence**, all the books both of the Old and the New Testaments. .. **as well as the traditions**, those pertaining to faith as well as those pertaining to morals, as having been prescribed either orally by Christ, or by the Holy Spirit, and having been preserved in the Catholic Church by continuous succession" (Council of Trent, Session IV, 1st Decree).

"We, the sacred Council approving, teach and so define as dogma divinely revealed that **the Roman Pontiff**, when he speaks **Ex Cathedra** – that is to say, when in the discharge of his supreme apostolic authority, he defines a doctrine

The Voice of Reformation

"1. We pledge ourselves to the prophetic and apostolic writings of the Old and New Testaments as the pure and clear fountain of Israel, which is the **only true norm according to which all teachers and teachings are to be judged and evaluated.**

2. Since in ancient time the true Christian doctrine as it was correctly and soundly understood was **drawn together out of God's Word** in brief articles or chapters against the aberrations of heretics, we further pledge allegiance of the three general Creeds, the Apostles, the Nicene, and the Athanasian, as the glorious confessions of the faith—succinct, Christian, and based upon the Word of God – in

1

The Voice of Rome:
regarding faith and morals to be held by the universal church—is, through the divine assistance promised to the blessed Peter himself, **possessed of the infallibility** with which the divine Redeemer willed that His Church should be endowed for defining doctrine concerning faith and morals; and that therefore such definitions of the Roman Pontiff are **of themselves, and not from the consent of the church, unalterable"** (Dogmatic constitution, "Pastor aeternus," Vatican Council, 1870, Session IV).

"40. Is Holy Scripture the only source of Christian doctrine? No, there is another source, and this is known as Tradition.

"41. What is Tradition? Tradition is the word of God not written in the Bible, but transmitted in unbroken succession, by word of mouth, from the Apostles to us.

"42. Where are the teachings of Tradition contained? In the decrees of councils, the acts of the Holy See, the liturgical books, the works of Christian art, and the writings of the Fathers and Doctors of the Church.

"43. Why is Tradition of equal authority with Holy Scripture? It is of equal authority, because it is equally the Word of God.

"44. To whom does the interpretation of Holy Scripture and of Tradition belong? To the infallible teaching authority of the Church, the guardian of revealed truth.

(Course of Religious Instruction; **Manual of Christian Doctrine**, 62nd Edition, LaSalle Bureau, Brothers of the Christian Schools, New York City, 1948). (Our emphases).

The Voice of Reformation
which all those heresies which at that time had arisen within the Christian church are clearly and solidly refuted.

3. By a special grace our merciful God has in these last days brought to light the truth of his word amid the abominable darkness of the papacy through the faithful ministry of that illustrious man of God, Dr. Luther. This doctrine, **drawn from and conformed to the Word of God**, is summarized in the articles and chapters of the Augsburg Confession against the aberrations of the papacy and of other sects. We therefore declare our adherence to the first, unaltered Augsburg Confession (in the form in which it was set down in writing in the year 1530 and submitted to Emperor Charles V at Augsburg by a number of Christian electors, princes, and estates of the Roman Empire as the common confession of the reformed churches) as our symbol in this epoch, **not because this confession was prepared by our theologians but because it is taken from the Word of God and solidly and well grounded therein.** This symbol distinguishes our reformed churches from the papacy and from other condemned sects and heresies. We appeal to it just as in the ancient church. It was traditional and customary for later synods and Christian bishops and teachers to appeal and confess adherence to the Nicene Creed." (**Formula of Concord,** Solid Declaration, Rule and Norm, 3-5). (Our emphases)

THE ISSUE AT A GLANCE

THIS?   OR   THIS?

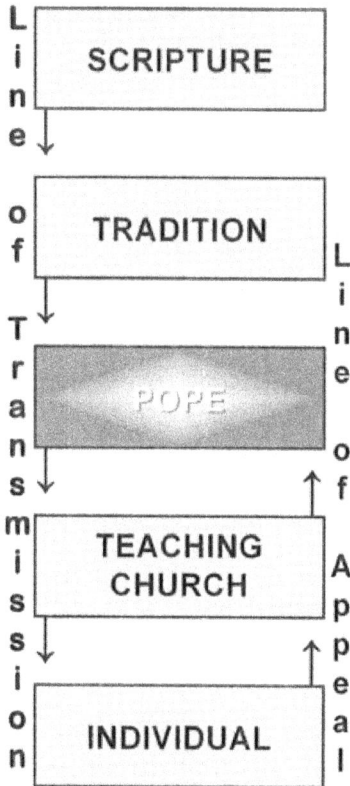

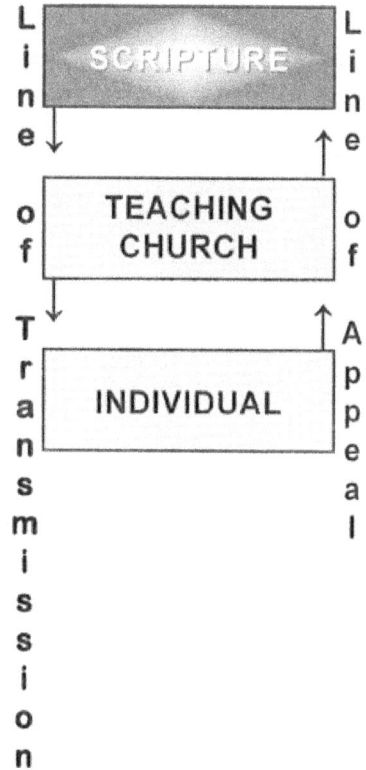

ABOVE: In the Roman scheme, Scripture is not directly available as source and norm of truth. It must first be completed by Tradition, and then get past the "filter" of the Pope, Note how similar this is to modern, Liberal theology, which also regards Scripture not as direct doctrinal substance, but as a "doctrinal basis", in other words, a flexible, waxen nose, to be twisted this way and that by the theological experts, who thus take the place of the Pope in modern Protestantism. Note also that there can be no appeal from or beyond the Pope, whose infallible definitions are of themselves irreformable and unalterable.

ABOVE: In the Evangelical scheme of things the clear, infallible, and sufficient Scripture, transmitted through the generations by the Church, is itself the only ultimate source and norm of Christian doctrine and practice. The individual Christian can and must appeal directly to Scripture. The teaching Church must be able and willing at all times to justify and demonstrate conclusively, from the Scriptures alone, all points of its teaching and practice. Beyond what can be clearly proved from Scripture, the Church cannot demand conscientious assent or obedience.

BELOW: Since the Pope is the ultimate and authoritative interpreter of both Scripture and Tradition, it is clear that the latter are really no authorities at all, since they can only mean what the Pope says they mean. He, then, not they, is the only real authority. A rule that must be ruled by another rule is, to that extent, not a rule. The Pope is the only real doctrinal rule, to the exclusion of Scripture and Tradition, which merely supply the outward trappings of legitimacy.

BELOW: As the Word of God, Scripture reigns supreme and alone as doctrinal authority. Human reason, experience, tradition, science, etc., do not judge scripture, but are judged by it.

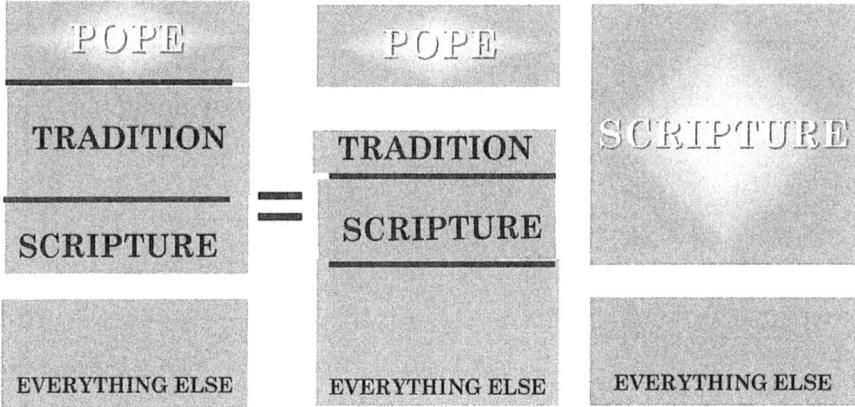

POPE	POPE	SCRIPTURE
TRADITION	TRADITION	
SCRIPTURE =	SCRIPTURE	
EVERYTHING ELSE	EVERYTHING ELSE	EVERYTHING ELSE

II. The Voice Of Scripture

(All quotations are from the official Roman Catholic Douay Version of Holy Scripture or from Monsignor Ronald Knox' translation, whichever seemed to express the original sense most clearly)

1. **Must Christians accept the teachings and directions of church authorities and officials simply on their own say so, without scripture proof, or do Christians have the right and the duty to question and judge all teachings and teachers on the basis of Scripture?**

St. Matthew 7:15: "Beware of false prophets, who come to you in the clothing of sheep, but inwardly they are ravening wolves."

(This necessarily implies

a. **Private Judgment** (quite different from "private interpretation"!), that is, the right and duty of personal conviction, of deciding for oneself whether something has been shown to be true or false, right or wrong, to the satisfaction of one's own conscience; and therefore

b. **An objective norm or standard**, above and beyond any and all ecclesiastical teachers, and directly accessible to all Christians; this, in post-Apostolic times, can only be Sacred Scripture

For as Luther put it so graphically: "If the sheep were not allowed to flee from the wolves until the wolves themselves, through their Christian Council and official decree, commanded the sheep to flee, the sheepfold would soon be empty and the shepherd would within one day find neither

4

milk, cheese, butter, wool, meat, nor even a hoof!"

St. Matthew 16:6 ff.: "Who said to them: Take heed and beware of the leaven of the Pharisees and Sadducees . . . Then they understood that he said not that they should beware of the leaven of bread, but of the doctrine of the Pharisees and Sadducees."

(Note that the people Christ warned against were not some little school of thought, but the highest official church authorities of their day!)

St. Matthew 20:25ff.: "You know that the princes of the Gentiles Lord it over them; and they that are the greater, exercise power upon them. It shall not be so among you."

Acts 17:11 "These were of a better breed than the Thessalonians; they welcomed the word with all eagerness, and examined the scriptures, day after day, to find out whether all this was true" (Knox).

I John 4:1: "Dearly beloved, believe not every spirit, but try the spirits if they be of God: because many false prophets are gone out into the world."

2. Does all this apply also to the Pope, or is he an exception – possessed of absolute, dictatorial powers over Christians and therefore entitled to a blind, unquestioning obedience not due to other teachers?

St. Matthew 16:18ff.: "Thou art Peter; and upon this rock I will build my Church, and the gates of hell shall not prevail against it. And I will give to thee the keys of the kingdom of heaven. And whatsoever thou shalt bind upon earth, it shall be bound also in heaven; and whatsoever thou shalt loose on earth, it shall be loosed also in heaven."

St. Matthew 18:18: "Amen I say to you, whatsoever you shall bind upon earth shall be bound also in heaven; and whatsoever you shall loose upon earth shall be loosed also in heaven."

Ephesians 2:20: "Built upon the foundation of the Apostles and Prophets, Jesus Christ Himself being the chief corner stone."

(Honestly now, is there one word in Matthew 16:18, 19 which teaches or even remotely suggests any idea of papal monarchy or infallibility? Note that in Matthew 16 Peter is promised nothing more than what the whole Christian Church is given in Matthew 18, and that in Eph. 2 Christ Himself is the Chief Corner Stone, Peter being simply a part of "the foundation of the Apostles and Prophets." Note also how these great Church Fathers understood the Matthew 16 passage:

St. Cyprian: "that which Peter was, were certainly also the other Apostles, endowed with an equal partnership both of honour and of authority" (**Of the Unity of the Catholic Church**, ch. 4 Migne, Patrology, Latin series, IV, 500).

St. Hilary: "The Father had revealed this to Peter, that he said 'You are the Son of the living God'. . . On this rock of confession the Church is built . . . This faith is the foundation of the Church" (**Of the Trinity**, VI, 34ff., Migne, **Patrology**, L.s.,X, 186ff).

St. Bede: "Figuratively He said to him: 'On this Rock,' that is, on the Saviour Whom you have confessed, the Church is built" (**Expla-**

nations of the Gospel of St. Matthew. Migne, **Patrology**, L.s.,XXXII, 618).

"Peter, as the one speaking for the others, one for all, said: 'You are the Christ, the Son of the living God' . . . not on Peter, which you are, but on the Rock, which you have confessed..." (**Treatise on the Gospel of St. John**, 124,21, Migne, **Patrology**, L.s., XXXVIII, 1238 ff.).

"On this faith, on that which was said: 'You are the Christ, the Son of the living God'. 'On this rock,' He said, 'I will build My Church'" (Migne, **Patrology**, L.S., XXX,2054).

"For the Rock was not so named after Peter, but Peter is named thus after the Rock, just as Christ is not named after the Christians, but the Christians after Christ. . . . On this Rock then, which you have confessed, I will build My Church, for the Rock was Christ, on which Foundation also Peter himself was built, for other foundation can no man lay that that which is laid which is Jesus Christ" (quoted in Boerhringer, Kirchengeschichte, 1/3, 339).

St. Matthew 23:8-10: "you are not to claim the title of Rabbi; you have but one Master, and you are all brethren alike. Nor are you to call any man on earth your father; you have but one Father, and he is in heaven. Nor are you to be called teachers; you have one teacher, Christ"(Knox).

I Corinthians 4:15: "Yes, you may have ten thousand schoolmasters in Christ, but not more than one father; it was I that begot you in Jesus Christ when I preached the Gospel to you" (Knox).

("Pope" of course means "Father." Note that Paul, not Peter, was the "one father" of the Corinthians, and not in the sense of rule, but in the sense that he had brought them the Gospel, which is the only instrument through which God creates spiritual life).

Acts 8:14: "And now the apostles at Jerusalem, hearing that Samaria had received the Word of God, sent Peter and John to visit them" (Knox).

I Corinthians 4:6: "That in us you may learn that one be not puffed up against the other for another above that which is written."

II Corinthians 11:5: "I claim to have done no less than the very greatest of the apostles" (Knox).

II Corinthians 12:11: "No, I have done no less than the very greatest of the apostles, worthless as I am" (Knox).

(Literally, according to the Greek text: "in nothing was I inferior to the foremost apostles." It is also clear from the whole context that it is a question of Paul's Apostolic status and authority, not of how much work he has done)

Galatians 2:6-15: "But of them who seemed to be something (what they were some time, it is nothing to me, God accepted not the person of man), for to me they that seemed to be some thing added nothing" (Douay). "On the contrary, those who were reputed to be the main support of the Church, James and Cephas, and John, saw plainly that I was commissioned to preach to the uncircumcised, as Peter was to the circumcised; he whose power had enabled Peter to become the apostle of the circumcised, had enabled me to become the apostle of the Gentiles. And

6

so, recognizing the grace God had given me, they joined their right hands in fellowship with Barnabas and myself; the Gentiles were to be our province, the circumcised theirs . . . Afterwards, when Cephas (Peter) came to Antioch, I opposed him openly; he stood self-condemned . . . The rest of the Jews were no less false to their principles. . . So, when I found that they were not following the true path of the gospel, I said to Cephas in front of them all, since thou, who are born Jew, dost follow the Gentile, not the Jewish way of life, but what right dost thou bind the Gentiles to live like Jews?" (Knox)

(According to this, if Peter was Pope, then only of the Jews, for the Gentiles were Paul's' province. If modern, non-Jewish Christians are to have a Pope, he must be the successor of Paul not of Peter! Note also that Paul knows nothing of Peter's supposed powers of legislating for the whole Church; for Paul expressly challenges Peter: "By what right dost thou bind the gentiles, etc.?")

St. John 5:31: "If I bear witness of Myself, my witness is not true."

(Of course the Lord's self-testimony was in and of itself inviolably true (St. John 8:14). But, speaking hypothetically. He evidently means to say: If you had only My own self-witness, without any corroborating testimony from anywhere else, you would be justified in rejecting it as false. But in addition to My own witness, there is the witness of John the Baptist (v. 33), of My own supernatural work (v. 36), of the Father Himself (v. 37), and of the Scriptures (v. 39).

What the Lord was willing, hypothetically, to apply even to Himself, must certainly hold for any mere man: If the Papacy is based only on self-witness, it is a fraud. Yet the whole Roman, Papal argument is nothing but a vicious circle of self-testimony: Accept me, because I say so!

But are not Scripture and Tradition also used as witnesses? No! They are dragged in for appearances' sake, but they cannot be cross-examined, as it were, in open court, as to their real meaning. Every question addressed to them is intercepted by the Papacy, replying in their behalf. When the Papacy says: "St. Matthew and St. Augustine teach papal infallibility," this has the Form of an appeal to Scripture and Tradition. In actual fact it means: "You must accept this as the teaching of St. Matthew and St. Augustine, because I am the official interpreter of Scripture and Tradition and I say so." A real appeal from the Papacy to Tradition or to Scripture is simply impossible in the self-serving Roman system, which therefore clearly suggests the following text:

II Thessalonians 2:3ff: "Let no man deceive you by any means, for unless there come a revolt first, and the man of sin be revealed, the son of perdition, who opposed and is lifted up above all that is called God or that is worshipped, so that he sitteth in the temple of God, shewing himself as if he were God."

(Pope Leo XIII, 1878-1903, declared in his **Praeclara Gratulatio-**

nis Publicae: "We hold upon this earth the place of God Almighty"!)

3. Is Holy Scripture A Clear And Sufficient Guide For Christian Faith And Life?

Isaiah 8:20 "To the law rather, and to the testimony. And if they speak not according to this word, they shall not have the morning light."

Psalm 118:105: "Thy Word is a lamp to my feet, and a light to my paths."

(A light which itself needs to be illuminated from some other source is a pretty dim and useless sort of light!)

St. Luke 16:29: "They have Moses and the prophets; let them listen to these" (Knox).

St. John 20:30-31: "There are many other miracles Jesus did in the presence of his disciples, which are not written down in this book; so much has been written down, that you may learn to believe Jesus is the Christ, the Son of God, and so believing find life through his name" (Knox).

(Note here St. Augustine's comment on St. John 16:12: "Since the Evangelists were silent, which of us will say that it was this or that; or if someone should dare to say it, how will he prove it? Who is so vain and presumptuous as to claim without a divine testimony—even if he should be speaking the truth—that it was this which the Holy Ghost did not wish to write through the Evangelists? Who of us would do this without casting himself into the greatest guilt of presumption, since he is possessed of neither Prophetic nor Apostolic status?")

Acts 17:11 "These were of a better breed than the Thessalonians; they welcomed the word with all eagerness, and examined the scriptures, day after day, to find out whether all this was true" (Knox).

II Corinthians 1:13: "And we mean by our letters nothing else than what you read in them, and understand us to mean" (Knox).

II Corinthians 4:3: "But if our Gospel be also hid, it is hid to them that are lost."

II Timothy 3:15-17: "And because from thy infancy thou hast known the Holy Scriptures, which can instruct thee to salvation, by the faith which is in Christ Jesus. All Scripture, inspired of God, is profitable to teach, to reprove, to correct, to instruct in justice that the man of God may be perfect, furnished of every good work."

(This is even more interesting when we reflect that "man of God" here and in I Timothy 6:11 means, most likely, a minister of the Church. It is therefore rendered as "God's servant" by Knox. The point then is that Scripture in itself supplies the servant of Christ and His Church with everything necessary for the good performance of the duties of his sacred Office!)

II Peter 1:20-21: "No prophecy in scripture is the subject of private interpretation" (Knox).

(This obviously means that no man--therefore also not the Pope — has the right to bind the Church to some arbitrary interpretation

8

which cannot be proved from the sacred text itself. Scripture must be allowed to interpret itself. This means that a good interpreter is one who can show that his interpretation is demanded by the grammar of the text itself, by the context, and by other clear Scripture texts which have a bearing on the matter. Lutherans have never claimed the right of private interpretation; rather, they have strongly rejected this as subjectivism. The Papacy on the other hand has always insisted that its private interpretations, for which there is no proof whatever, must be accepted unquestioningly by the rest of Christendom!

Very different from **Private Interpretation**, that is, an arbitrary reading of things into the text rather than out of it, is **Private Judgment**, which is commanded in all the many texts which expect Christians to distinguish truth from falsehood).

III. Voices From Tradition

(Most of the quotations from the Church Fathers which follow are taken from the magnificent collection found in Martin Chemnitz' Examen, a brilliant 16th century analysis and refutation of the Roman Catholic Council of Trent. This monumental work has never been successfully answered).

St. Irenaeus: "The Apostles at that time preached the Gospel, but later by the will of God handed it down to us in the Scriptures, as the future round and pillar of our faith" (**Against the Heresies**, Book 3, ch. 1).

St. Augustine: "In that which is openly stated in Scripture, everything is found comprising faith and manner of life, namely hope and charity" (**Christian Doctrine**, Book 2, ch. 9).

"If anyone should teach you, concerning either Christ or His Church, or anything whatsoever pertaining to faith and life--I will not say, if we, but what Paul has added: if an angel from Heaven should teach you anything beyond what you have received in the Scriptures of the Law and the Gospel, let him be accursed!" (**Against The Letters of Petilian**, Book 3, ch. 6).

"What more can I teach you than what we read in the Apostle? For the Holy Scripture has fixed a rule for our doctrine, so that we dare not be wiser than we ought to be. It is not for me therefore to teach you anything else, except to explain to you the words of the Teacher" (**The Benefit of the Unmarried State**, ch. 1).

St. Athanasius: "The holy and divinely inspired Scriptures suffice for the entire instruction in the truth" (**Against the Pagans**).

"The books of the Old and New Testaments are the wells of salvation . . . . . in these alone the doctrine of true religion is proclaimed. Let no one add to them nor take away anything from them" (**Festal Epistles**).

"As you desire, we will give a brief exposition of the Christian Faith, which, indeed you might have found from the divine oracles. For, indeed, the holy and inspired Scriptures are sufficient of themselves to make known the truth" (**Against Arianism** I,8).

St. John Chrysostom: "Everything is clear and plain from the divine

9

Scriptures: whatever is necessary is crystal-clear (**Manifesta**)" (On II Thessalonians 2).

St. Jerome: "The Holy Spirit's doctrine is that which is revealed in the canonical Scriptures, and if Councils decide anything contrary to them, I regard it as a crime" (**On Galatians**).

"As we accept those things which are written, so we reject those things which are not written" (**Against Helvius**).

Beyond Scripture - Sin!

St. Basil: "If the Lord is faithful in all His words, and all His commandments are faithful, then it is a manifest falling away from faith and criminal arrogance, either to reject anything of what is written, or to add anything of what is not written; for Christ said: My sheep hear My voice, but another they will not follow, but flee, for they do not know his voice."

"Wherefore I exhort and beseech you to refrain from useless enquiries, and unseemly contention about words, and to be satisfied with what is said by the sacred writers and the Lord Himself" (**Confession of Faith**).

"Those who are instructed in the Scriptures ought to test the things that are taught by their teachers, and to receive what agrees with the Scriptures and to reject what is contrary."

"What is the characteristic feature of the believer? Not to dare to add anything; for if everything which is not of faith is sin but faith cometh by hearing, and hearing by the Word of God, then everything which is outside the divinely inspired Scripture is sin, because it is not of faith" (**Morals**, 72,1; 80,22).

"We do not hold that it is fair to make the custom prevailing among them the law and rule of the right doctrine. Therefore the divinely inspired Scripture is made the umpire by us..." (**80th Epistle**).

"Believe those things which are written: the things that are not written, seek not" (**39th Homily**).

Lactantius: "Those things can have no foundation or firmness which are not sustained by any oracle of God's Word...The faith consists of that which is contained in the divine Scriptures" (Book 5, ch. 4).

Even Councils Not Binding
Without Scripture

St John Chrysostom: "They claim concerning Paradise, that it is to be understood not according to what is written, but otherwise. But if Scripture wants to teach us anything like that, then it explains itself, and does not let the hearer err. I beg and plea therefore that, shutting our ears to everything else, we may follow the plumb-line and rules of the Sacred Scripture" (**13th Homily on Genesis**).

St. Cyril: "It is necessary for us to follow divine Scriptures, and in nothing to deviate from what they prescribe" (**Concerning the right faith**).

St. Augustine: "But now neither may I bring up the Nicene Council, nor you the Arminian, as having decided in advance. Neither will I be bound by the authority of the former, nor you by that of the latter. According to the authorities of Scripture, not according to any sort of special witnesses, but according to the common witnesses recognized by both sides, let issue compete with issue, cause with cause, argument with argument" (**Against Maximinus**, Book 3, chapter 14).

Origen: "It is necessary for us to call the Holy Scriptures to the witness-and for our own ideas and interpretations without these witnesses do not find faith" (**Commentary on Jeremiah**).

St. Jerome: "Without the authority of the Scriptures, talkativeness does not find faith" (**Commentary on Titus**).

"What has no authority from the Scriptures, is condemned with the same ease with which it is accepted" (**On St. Matthew, Chapter 23**).

Scripture ONLY Refuge

St. John Chrysostom: "When you shall see the impious heresy, which is the army of Antichrist, standing in the holy places of the Church, then let those who are in Judaea flee to the hills, that is, let those who are in Christendom flee to the Scriptures. For the true Judaea is Christendom, and the mountains are the Scriptures of the Prophets and Apostles, as it is written: His foundations are in the holy mountains. But why must all Christians at that time flee to the Scriptures? Because at that time, when heresy shall have taken over the churches, there will be no other possible proof of true Christianity, no other possible refuge for the Christians, desiring to recognize the truth of the faith, except the divine Scriptures. Before it was shown in many ways, which was the true Church of Christ, where will he recognize it, in such a confusion of similarity, except solely and alone through the Scriptures? The Lord therefore, knowing that such a confusion of affairs would arise in the last days, commands that the Christians who are in Christendom, and who wish to attain to the firmness of true faith, should flee to nothing else except to the Scriptures. If they pay attention to anything else, they will be offended and perish, not understanding which is the true Church, and thereby falling into the abomination of desolations which stands in the holy places of the Church" (**49th Homily**, on St. Matthew 24).

St. Augustine: "Let our writings depart from our midst, let the Book of God come into the centre. Hear Christ speaking, hear Truth talking" (On Psalm 57).

"Where there is a dispute about a very obscure matter, not supported by certain and clear proofs from the divine Scriptures, human preconception must restrain itself and not go off on one side or the other" (**Of the Merits of Sinners**, Book 2, Chapter 36).

St. John Chrysostom: "If anything is spoken without Scripture, the devotion of the hearers limps. But where the testimony has proceeded from the Scripture of God's Word, it strengthens both the sermon of the speaker and the soul of the hearer" (On Psalm 95).

"Whatever is required for salvation, is already quite complete in the

Scriptures" (On St. Matthew 22).

Clear Scripture – Not "Follow the Leader"!

"We don't want to have the opinions of many, but let us investigate the issues themselves. For it is absurd not to believe others in money-matters, but to count and calculate for oneself, but then in much more important matters simply to follow the opinion of others, especially when we have the most exact balance, indicator, and rule, indeed the declaration of divine laws. I therefore pray you all that you would let go of what seems right to this one or to that one, and settle all this from the Scriptures" (13th Homily, on II Corinthians).

Origen: "As evidence for all words which we employ in matters of doctrine we must adduce the sense of Scripture, as confirming the sense we are expounding. For as all the gold which was outside the Temple was not sanctified, so every sense which is outside the divine Scripture, no matter how admirable it may seem to some, is not holy, because it is not contained in the sense of Scripture. Therefore we may not adduce our own thoughts for the confirmation of doctrine, unless it has been shown that they are for the confirmation of doctrine, unless it has been shown that they are holy, from the fact that they are contained in the divine Scriptures, as in the temples of God" (**25th Homily on St. Matthew**).

St. Cyril: "In order that the teachings of Scripture might be understandable to all, small and great, they have been usefully committed to familiar language, so that they do not exceed anyone's ability to comprehend" (**Against Julian**, Book 7)

St. Augustine: "Because in the Scriptures much is put figuratively and obscurely, let us mark out what is clear and obvious. For if this were not found in the Holy Scriptures, there would be no way of opening what is closed, and illuminating what is dark. We must therefore leave aside for the moment what is darkly put and wrapped in the veils of figurative language, and what can be interpreted both in our favour and in theirs" (**Against Petilian**, Ch. 5).

"Let them not gather and harp on the things said obscurely or ambiguously or figuratively, which everyone interprets as he pleases, in accord with his own sense. For such passages cannot be rightly understood and explained unless those which are completely clear are first grasped in firm faith" (Ch. 16).

"Produce something that does not need an interpreter, and from which it won't be proved to you that it deals with something else and that you are trying to twist it in favour of your meaning" (IBID).

"What is expressed ambiguously, and can be interpreted both in our favour and in yours, does not help your cause at all, but plainly supports bad cause only by drawing it out...These are mystical, hidden, figurative passages; we demand something obvious, which doesn't need an interpreter" (Ch 19).

St. Ambrose: "He speaks with us in such a manner that we understand his speech" (Book 3, Letter 5).

"Paul in most of his communications so explains himself, that he who deals with them finds nothing of his own to add, and if he wishes to say something, must exercise the office of grammarian more than that of debater" (Book 2, Letter 7).

Lactantius: "Should God, the Author of mind and voice and language not have been able to speak clearly? Indeed, the supreme Providence wishes those things which are divine to be without rouge, so that all might understand what He Himself has said to all."

No Self-Witness – Only Scripture

St. Augustine: "Let us not hear: 'I say this', 'you say that,' but: 'Thus saith the Lord'. Since it is the Lord's books to the authority of which we both submit, and which we both believe, let us there seek the Church, there settle our case..."

"Away from our midst whatever we quote against one another not from the canonical divine books but from elsewhere! Someone may perhaps ask: 'Why do you want these removed from our midst?' Because I do not want the holy Church proved with human examples, but with the divine oracles...

"Whatever they may adduce, and from wherever they may quote, let us rather, if we are His sheep, hear the voice of our Shepherd. Therefore let us seek the Church in the canonical Holy Scriptures...

"Read us this out of the Law, the Prophets, the Psalms, the Gospel, read it from the letters of the Apostles, and we will believe it...

"One may not agree even with the Catholic bishops if they perhaps err somewhere and decide something contrary to the canonical Scriptures of God...

"Whoever proclaims anything else, let him be accursed – or let him read it to me from the Holy Scriptures, and he shall not be accursed...

"Let them, if they can, prove their church, not with the words and applause of the Africans, not with councils of their own bishops, not with the writings of various controversialists, not with lying signs and wonders – for against these very things we have been prepared and cautioned by the Word of the Lord – but with what the Law prescribes, with the prediction of the Prophets, with songs of the Psalms, with the Voice of the Shepherd Himself, with the words and works of the Evangelists, that is with all the canonical authorities of the Sacred Books...

"For neither do we ourselves ask anyone to believe that we are in the Church of Christ because innumerable bishops of our communion recommend the Church to which we hold, or because she is proclaimed by the councils of our colleagues, or because throughout the world in the holy places frequented by our communion such miraculous answers to prayers or healings occur, etc...

"Not because Ambrose of Milan is in her, not because she is proclaimed as such by the Councils of our Church, or because in her holy places great miracles of answered prayer or healing occur, or because this one had vision or that one a trance...Whatever of this sort happens in the catholic Church; but the catholic Church is not proved to be such because this sort of things happens in her. The law and the Prophets and the Gospels and their statements –that is the true testimony. Everything else is the smoke of earthly trick-flares compared to this thunder and lightning from above...

"Demand of them that they show some clear testimonies from the canonical books. Remember that it is a word of the Lord: 'They have Moses and the Prophets, let them hear them!'" (**Of the Unity of the Church**, chapters 3, 6, 10, 12, 16, 20).

IV. CONCLUDING NOTE

We know of course that there are in the Church Fathers beside these splendid sayings also statements which, when twisted (II Peter 3:16!), can be made to appear to support the modern Roman Catholic notions about Tradition and Church authority. Naturally one also finds in antiquity the beginnings of the false view of Tradition. The decisive fact however is the obvious one that the above quotations could not have been written by people who accepted the Tridentine and Vatican Councils. There is here a fundamental unbridgeable gulf between old Church Fathers who could write like that, and modern Rome, which can't.

In view of this clear evidence from the Church Fathers it may be asked why Rome has, since the Reformation, been so insistent on the idea that Scripture alone is not enough, that it must be supplemented by Tradition, and that both must be unconditionally subject to what amounts to "private interpretation" by the Papacy, which thus acts as a kind of filter, having absolute control over how much of Scripture and Tradition can "get through," and in what form! The only convincing answer to this question is suggested by history:

At Augsburg, in 1530, when the Evangelical princes and estates had presented their Confession to Emperor Charles V, the Roman Catholic Duke William of Bavaria asked Dr. John Eck, one of Luther's chief opponents, whether he could refute the Confession. Dr. Eck replied that he could do so from the Church Fathers, but not from the Scriptures alone! The Duke's classic comeback: "So I hear then that the Lutherans sit in the Scriptures, and we sit outside!"

Also at Augsburg, Stadion, the Roman Catholic bishop of that city, said about the Lutheran Confession: "What has been read to us is the pure truth of the Gospel and we cannot deny it!"

The sixteenth century Roman Catholic author Pighius says in his treatise **Of the Hierarchy of the Church**: "If we had been mindful of this principle, namely that heretics are not to be corrected and convinced from Scripture, our cause would undoubtedly have fared better. But because, in order to demonstrate their cleverness and learning, people allowed themselves to be drawn into a controversy with Luther on the basis of Scripture, there has arisen the conflagration which we now behold to our sorrow..." (chapter 4).

This of course is rather like saying, in the middle of the game: "We can't win by the old rules—let's change them!"

Christians today must still choose between the old religion of the Scriptures and the great Church Fathers, upheld by the Reformation, and the new religion of the Roman Papacy which insists on being a law unto itself and refuses to let itself be judged by the old Christian standards!

Christian News, September 16, 1968

1. Rome venerates all the books of the Old and New Testaments as well as ____.
2. What did Vatican II say about the Pope? ____
3. What does Rome say about Tradition? ____
4. Where are the teachings of Tradition contained?____
5. The Voice of the Reformation says that the only true norm is ____.
6. The three general creeds are based on ____.
7. The Augsburg Confession is taken from ____.
8. All quotations from the Bible are from ____.
9. Is there one word in Matthew 16:18, 19 which suggests any idea of papal monarchy or infallibility? ____
10. Who is the Chief Cornerstone? ____
11. How did the great Church fathers understand Matthew 16?____
12. "Pope" means ____.
13. The whole Roman papal argument is nothing but ____.
14. What did Pope Leo XIII declare? ____
15. Scripture must be allowed to ____itself.
16. Have Lutherans claimed the right of private interpretation? ____
17. What is Martin Chemnitz's Examen? ____
18. What does tradition say about tradition? ____
19. Even Council is not binding without ____.
20. Rome today says ____ is not enough but must be supplemented by ____.
21. Roman Catholic Duke William of Bavaria said: "So I hear then that the Lutherans sit in the ____, and we sit ____ ."
22. Christians today must choose between the old religion of ____ and the new religion of____.

"HELSINKI, DOCTRINAL UNITY, AND JUSTIFICATION"

Marquart Advises Australians to avoid Lutheran Federation — Claims LWF Tolerates Bultmann's denials of historic Christianity

(Rev. Kurt Marquart is the pastor of the Evangelical Lutheran Parish of Toowoomba, Australia. He attended the Fourth Assembly of the Lutheran World Federation in Helsinki as an observer for Lutheran News.)

This essay answers those who have charged that Lutheran News misrepresented the Helsinki Assembly when it reported that the Assembly failed to reach agreement on the fundamental doctrine of justification by faith alone. Various Lutheran officials in this country have reported that the disagreement was only a matter of theological formulations. Ed.

The trouble with this typical son of the manse, said Reinhold Niebuhr once about the American President Woodrow Wilson, is that he "believes too much in words."

This habit of mistaking words for realities can be counted on, no doubt, to assure general acceptance of the Lutheran World Federation's current claim that its Helsinki Assembly agreed on the doctrine of Justification. "ASSEMBLY ACTION ON JUSTIFICATION HELD NO SIGN OF DOCTRINAL DISUNITY" is the heading of an official release (No. 31/63, September 12, 1963) of the L.W.F.'s *Geneva News Bureau.*

I.

Before listing a few items to show that doctrinal unity did not in fact prevail at Helsinki, we must examine some of the historical reasons why such unity was quite impossible.

The fact of the matter is that the clergy of the territorial churches of Lutheran Europe (the Scandinavian countries and parts of Germany) are trained at state owned universities, over which the churches can and do exercise no effective doctrinal control ever! The rule that prevails at these universities is: "Gleichberechtigung der Richtungen" (equal rights for all points of view). If Professor X wishes to be conservative, that is his privilege, if only he is scholarly about it. But if Professor Y, in the name of scholarship, wishes to reject the Trinity, the Incarnation, the Divinity of Christ, the Virgin Birth, the Atonement and the Resurrection—as Prof. Bultmann, for example, has been doing for decades—then this too is perfectly acceptable. What sort of theological convictions can future pastors be expected to acquire in this atmosphere?

Critical Bible Approach Rules

But, someone might ask: Are these radical, liberal views, which attack the foundations of the Christian Faith, really widespread? Unfortunately, yes. And here is why: Two centuries ago Rationalism took possession of Protestant European university theology. What is Rationalism?

It is the notion that human reason is supreme, that it, and not Scripture, decides what is true and what is not. Naturally, Rationalism did away with all the mysteries and the supernatural truths of Christianity. It is true that other movements, including a religious and Confessional revival, swept Europe after Rationalism. But it is not true that Rationalism is dead. It is very much alive. It has merely changed its form several times. The "scientific," critical approach to Scripture, which is the soul of Rationalism, continues to rule, practically unchallenged, throughout the domains of the established university theology.

Dr. W. Oesch, who is perhaps the leading Confessional Lutheran theologian in the world today, has, on the basis of his own vast knowledge and experience of the situation, given this penetrating description of the theological complexion of Lutheran Europe:

"There was an increase in the earnestness of preaching after the Hitler era, and there always has been, for more than a hundred years, quite a number of pastors, even in union church-bodies, who preached Lutheran Law-and-Gospel sermons. There were, and are, even wonderful men like Laache. But side by side with them continues to stand, as in the past, the apostate section of the clergy, who believe neither in the Triune God, nor in the Incarnation, nor in the Resurrection, nor in any other saving truth. To be sure, outspoken radicals are not frequent in the top office; but this is due to their vulnerability (i.e. their openness to attacks from conservative quarters), and hence to political rather than theological considerations" ("A Lutheran Appraisal of the Church Situation in Germany," Kaiserslautern, August 11-12, 1959).

The trouble is that modern Rationalism disguises itself in the words and language of Scripture. The very learned Dr. Gustaf Wingren, professor of theology at the University of Lund, Sweden, writes:

"Barth has the ability to a very large degree of being able to employ the language of scripture in a system that is totally foreign to the Bible" (*Theology in Conflict*, p. 125).

A Fable to Pacify the Gullible

That "neo-orthodoxy", or Barthianism, has given up the anti-Scriptural Rationalism of the older liberalism, is a fable invented to pacify the gullible. A modern-theological authority, *A Handbook of Christian Theology*, admits:

"Neo-orthodoxy agrees with liberalism that the whole area of spatio-temporal fact and event is the valid object of scientific inquiry, with the result that the hypotheses of science in the area of natural and historical fact are regarded as authoritative...Likewise, although the Incarnation has become the central theological doctrine of all neo-orthodoxy, the factual manifestations and explanations of the Incarnation (e.g. the miracles, the Virgin Birth, and the Empty Tomb) have not played such a central role in contemporary theology as they did in 'orthodoxy'. In other words, to the contemporary thinker theological doctrines are statements

17

containing symbolic rather than literal truth, propositions pointing to the religious dimensions of events rather than propositions containing factual information about events...The intricate relation between the historic fact and the religious, 'mythical' or symbolical interpretation of the fact remains as an important and as yet unsolved problem for neo-orthodoxy."

No Revealed Truth

Gustaf Aulen, a bishop in the Church of Sweden, former professor at Lund, and a former leader in the Lutheran World Federation , is regarded, together with Anders Nygren, as leader of that influential neo-Lutheranism known as "Lundensian theology". The informed student cannot read Aulen's major work, *The Faith of the Christian Church*, without realizing that it represents a thinly veiled Liberalism, which rejects the divine authority of Scripture and denies that any such thing as "true doctrine" is even available to the Church. There simply is no such thing as God-given, revealed truth or doctrine; "theology" merely tries to find truth as best it can, but all its statements are only symbolical! The doctrines of the Trinity, the Divinity of Christ, and the Atonement (specially treated in *Christus Victor*) are "reinterpreted" so radically, that the result can only be described as heresy, in fact, apostasy from the Christian Faith.

And then there is Rudolf Bultmann, who thinks that if the Bible is to be presented to "modern man," it must first be freed from such "mythological elements" as the Virgin Birth, the Divinity and Pre-Existence of Christ, the Atonement, and the Resurrection! Please study carefully the following statements of Dr. Lilje, in which he expresses regret that this heretical "theology" has not penetrated more deeply into the congregations, as well as hope that it will do so in the future:

"The upheavals which took place in scientific theology within the last three decades belong to the great spiritual revolutions in church history. With the rise of Karl Barth there has begun a new chapter in theology. At this moment he is probably the greatest living theologian...The great critical rethinking introduced into New Testament exegesis by Rudolf Bultmann enjoys worldwide recognition today. It has increasingly given direction to research in all parts of the world. The more impartially and objectively one views this new orientation of theological endeavor, the more distressing naturally will be the realization that congregations are not affected by what is happening...The question as to what the word of revelation within the traditional Biblical Word can tell us has been lifted to a completely new basis... A movement for a new theology which has penetrated to the foundation will also find the language that can be understood by the congregation and which, under God's Holy Spirit, can turn into genuine movements for renewal of the Church" (*Evangelical Digest*, September, 1959).

Now, who is Dr. Lilje? Is he some insignificant extremist somewhere in Ethiopia? No, he is one of the most important personages in world "Lutheranism". As Bishop of Hannover, Germany, he is head of the Hannoverian State Church. He is past president of the Lutheran World Federation, and is still one of its most influential leaders. He figured prominently at Helsinki, where he served as chairman of the committee which was to summarize the discussions on Justification, but failed, despite two attempts, to produce a document acceptable to the Assembly!

Disagreement—Simply Verbal?

And the most recent past president of the L.W.F., Dr. Franklin Clark Fry, who presided at Helsinki, is the president of the "Lutheran Church in America," which tolerates radical liberals such as Joseph Sittler, who not only denies the divine authority of Scripture (*The Doctrine of the Word*, 1948), but has even questioned the real Divinity and personal preexistence of Christ ("*A Christology of Function,*" *Lutheran Quarterly,*" May, 1954). In 1961, Muhlenberg Press, official publishing house of that church, published a book, *Conversation on Faith*, which pretends to modernize the Christian message, but in reality surrenders it. The book denies the Trinity. Of Christ we read that "he was only a man and a creature who lived solely by the love of God" (p. 94), that the Virgin Birth was a "figurative, childlike interpretation" (p. 104), that we need not worry about "some external side of the resurrection message" (p. 128), that the Ascension is "based on the ancient mythical view of the world," and that it is "wrong...to think that the cross of Christ is a matter of reconciling God with a bloody sacrifice" (p. 119).

With this background information in mind, we are in a position to evaluate objectively the claim, advanced also in circles that should know better, that the disagreements in Helsinki were only apparent, being due to differences of opinion about what sort of language would best express the old truths in a fresh, modern, appealing, "relevant" way. The exact opposite was actually the case. It is not the disagreements but the agreements which were merely apparent! The trouble with Helsinki was not so much that people were saying different things in different ways, but rather that many were saying different things in the same way! Theological scholarship, can be—and is being—used today to convey practically any content. Try to imagine an "agreement" by, say, Menzies and Khrushchev, that there should be "freedom, democracy, equality, peace, and social progress for all peoples," which to one would mean the extension of our free way of life throughout the globe, while the other would be thinking of the universal extension of, say, Hungary's "workers' paradise"! This example will give one some idea of how meaningless loosely worded theological "agreements" are nowadays, even if the very terms of the Apostles' Creed are used!

II.

The following facts, which are by no means the only ones that could be cited, completely explode any claim that the disagreements about Justification were only verbal, and not doctrinal:

19

1. The Official Documents

In the December, 1961, number of the *Australasian Theological Review*, Dr. H. Hamann, Sr., analyzed a number of preliminary essays, on Justification, some by members of the L.W.F's Commission on Theology, which had appeared in the *Lutheran World*, the official organ of the LWF. We do not wish to repeat the many quotes cited by Dr. Hamann. Suffice it to say that these quotes constitute shocking evidence that not only Justification, but even the doctrines of the Trinity and of the Divinity of Christ are being undermined.

The official documents distributed at the Helsinki Assembly itself, also reveal not merely verbal, but doctrinal flaws and conflicts.

The first main lecture, *"Grace for the World,"* was delivered by Dr. Gerhard Gloege. The doctrine of justification presented in this paper was couched in philosophical terms and was far from clear. Some statements suggest universalism, and were so understood in some of the discussion groups. The heart of the Biblical, Reformation doctrine, that in which it differs from the Roman view, is that justification is not an internal improvement in man (that's sanctification) but God's judicial ("forensic") act, outside of man, declaring the sinner forgiven, and imputing to him the righteousness of Another, namely Christ's. All this, is, to say the least, rendered highly questionable by such statements as: "The old alternative whether the sinner is considered justified only in God's judgment—'forensically'— or whether he is actually justified— 'effectively' —is begging the question... The contrast between 'imputed' and 'real' justification...is outmoded as a result of the strictly theological definition of justification" (pp. 13 & 18). One also remembers that Dr. Gloege is the author of a book on Bultmann's programme of "demythologization," which while criticizing Bultmann, in some respects even quite fundamentally, nevertheless admits that there is mythology in the Bible, which must be dealt with somehow (*Mythologic und Luthertum, Recht und Grenze der Entmythologisierung*).

Dangerous Heresies

The official, printed statement on Justification, issued by the Commission on Theology, suggests some dangerous heresies, mainly of the modern-liberal variety. The following references are to the German version of the document, as translated by the undersigned:

"Today we cannot lightly dismiss the theological doctrine of the Roman Church as manifestly false, unbiblical, and unevangelical" (p. 6).

"While the Reformers regarded the message of the Bible as a unitary, almost monolithic affair, we today see a far greater variety and difference among the biblical writers. The Reformers believed that Justification was the theme which dominated the entire New Testament. Today we recognize that Justification is indeed one image which appears in the earliest Christian tradition, but only as one image among many...Can we continue to maintain that the article of Justification is the articulus stantis et cadentis ecclesiae (the article by which the Church either stands or falls), if already in the earliest period of the Church's life the possibility existed to proclaim the Gospel without reference to it?" (p. 7)

"But the critical study of Scripture suggests still more serious and insistent questions... Can the Old Testament, as we understand it in the light of thorough literary and historical studies, endure the kind of interpretation which it was given by the first disciples?" (p. 8) (We are tempted to ask: How can any Lutheran endure such attacks upon the Apostles of Christ?)

A Pet Notion — Man Has No Soul

On p. 19 there appears a paragraph which can only be understood as favoring the pet notion of modern theology, that man has no soul! The evolutionary origin of man and the evolutionary understanding of the Old Testament seems everywhere to be taken for granted. Justification is treated as one of many "images," rather than as the central reality of Scripture. While some striking formulations occur, which, if given orthodox interpretations, are quite good, the discussion is vague and inexact. "Certain orthodox Lutherans" are cited as examples of "self-righteousness," by virtue of their strict doctrinal convictions (pp. 25-26), but one looks in vain for any warning against the self-righteousness of modern theologians who exalt themselves above the authority of Christ and His Apostles!

Some of the most shocking statements appear in the printed report entitled *Department of Theology*. For example:

"There was rather quick agreement that justification is not the completely dominating theme of the New Testament. It is one of the pictures...It follows directly therefore that the doctrine of justification, even if it is a pure exegesis, can never claim to be the only pure exegesis" (p. 15). The pamphlet, which is the official report of both the Department of Theology and the Theological Commission, calmly continues by asserting three differences between the Reformation doctrine of justification and the teaching of the New Testament. For example:

"The New Testament does not know the idea of simul justus et peccator (Luther's phrase, meaning "at the same time both righteous and sinner". K.M.) A Christian is 'holy' and not a 'sinner'. Although both Paul and John deny that the baptismal man is completely free from sin, a consciousness of sin in the Reformation sense which calls for a permanent posture of repentance is foreign to them" (p. 16).

Conflict—Painfully Obvious

The damaging implications of these sentences are too strong to be neutralized by the talk about "differences of emphasis" on the following page of the pamphlet. And we know that modern theology has a habit of regarding the most hopeless contradictions as but different aspects of the same truth. The Gospel, doctrine, or "confession" is the same; only the interpretation, or "theological approach" is different, as Dr. Fry told the Assembly reassuringly, when the doctrinal conflict over Justification had become most painfully obvious!

21

Perhaps the most dangerous statement in the entire report occurs on page 18: "The statements about the pre-existence of Christ and the Trinity are nothing more than interpretations of the basic soteriological statement 'God was in Christ for our salvation'." And the previous sentence asserted that the ancient Creeds were concerned not with "metaphysics" but with "soteriology."

It is true that the alarming consequences of these assertions seem to be rejected in later statements on that page. It is also true, however, that documents prepared by committees often permit contradictory interpretations on certain points, and sometimes actually include contradictory formulations, reflecting the conflicting positions of their respective authors. At any rate, what is the meaning of that passage, if it is not intended to convey what the more radical type of modern theology would mean by exactly those expressions, namely that it does not matter very much whether Christ is really (that is what is meant by "metaphysics") the eternal, pre-existing Second Person of the Trinity; all that matters is that we find our "salvation" ("soteriology"!) in him, all else being mere "interpretation"?

2. The Discussions in Helsinki

Vatican Council (I & II) Fathers may have to hide their disagreements by pretending to argue only about the "opportuneness" of a certain definition. No such necessity restricted the tolerant, scientific theologians of Helsinki.

The undersigned clearly remembers encountering doctrinal differences during the discussion of justification by the discussion groups. The forensic, judical aspect of Justification, for example, was criticized as suggesting too much the atmosphere of the courtroom. Our notes record Bishop Lilje's reference, during the open hearing chaired by him, to "so many fundamental differences" which must somehow be dealt with. And Prof. Dr. Sommerlath asked reproachfully, possibly on the same occasion: "What does Justification mean? Do we really know that ourselves?"

One of the most dramatic incidents of the Assembly occurred when the conservative Bishop Bo Giertz, second vice-president of the L.W.F., emphatically attacked some of the more blatant statements in the printed Department of Theology reports (see quote above). The Bishop said that such statements, which attacked the very first principles of the Reformation, could not be tolerated. It is amusing to compare this incident with the version given in the official minutes (Saturday, August 3, 1963):

"It was moved from the floor that the Section on Theology be requested to study particularly certain statements on page 16 (English version) of the report of the Department of Theology (Document No. 7) which seem ambiguous."

"Ambiguous," when last heard of, meant "unclear"!

Doctrinal Disagreement

A motion to adopt Bishop Lilje's Report on the Discussion on the Theme "Justification" was overwhelmingly defeated, and so was a motion

22

to refer the report to the churches for discussion and comment. Finally the Assembly referred the document (Revised document no. 75) to the Commission on Theology, to do with as that body might deem proper. During the debate in connection with this matter, several speakers said that as Lutheran bishops and theologians they could not subscribe to such a statement. That clearly implied doctrinal, not merely verbal disagreement! Perhaps the most forthright and courageous testimony was given by Bishop Jacobi of Oldenburg (member of the L.W.F., and an official delegate), who said that to adopt the report would mean to encourage atheism and skepticism. The Bishop proposed a number of doctrinal corrections, but the chairman. Dr. Fry, announced: "Your three minutes are up!"

At a press-conference, attended by this observer, Dr. Fry was asked why the more radical theologians, like Bultmann, were not present at Helsinki. He replied that a ten-day Assembly was not equipped to cope with the chaos that would ensue, were the more radical thinkers present. This, though not the exact wording, was the sense of Dr. Fry's reply. It indicates that the L.W.F. leadership tried, as far as possible, to give the Assembly a "moderate" complexion. This must be kept in mind when considering the question in how representative the Helsinki Assembly was of the Federation's membership as a whole. It must also not be forgotten that the L.W.F. is intensively wooing The Lutheran Church—Missouri Synod, because the absence of that body, and its confessional sister churches throughout the world, maintains an embarrassingly obvious question mark on the face of the Federation's "Lutheranism".

Bultmann Would Be Welcome

Even so, some radicals appear to have slipped into the Assembly. In a discussion group devoted to the consideration of the proposed constitutional amendments, the undersigned asked what the practical meaning of the inclusion, in the doctrinal basis, of the Ecumenical Creeds would be. Would it mean that some one of Bultmann's views, for whom the Athanasian Creed is nothing but mythology, could not in any sense officially represent the L.W.F.? If it didn't mean that, what did it mean? The group chairman saw the difficulty, but replied that the Federation was so constituted that if Bultmann had been sent by a member church, and had cared to come, he would have been perfectly welcome at Helsinki. And, after all, wouldn't it be very interesting to have Prof. Bultmann present? There upon a young American spoke up and said: "Do you really think that Bultmann isn't here? I've talked to a number of people here who believe what Bultmann believes!"

3. Printed Reports

On August 4, 1963, the *New York Times* printed a special dispatch from its Helsinki correspondent, which included the following:

"Remarks on 'the depravity of man' by a conservative Lutheran leader from the United States were dismissed by an American youth as 'a lot of baloney'... Aside from semantics, a tour of the discussion groups indicated

23

the existence of some differing views of the central Lutheran doctrine and of some uncertainties. This doctrine, called 'justification by faith,' holds that salvation is granted by God to those who believe in Christ's atonement for their sins, and that good works are an outgrowth of this.

"Some discussion participants indicated their belief that Lutherans should give a far more prominent role to good deeds. To some conservative Lutherans, however, this appeared tinged with a concept similar to a Roman Catholic call for deeds as part of a procedure toward justification.

"One Scandinavian Lutheran suggested that, since the doctrine of justification divided churches, some other concept should be adopted as a central doctrine, to spur unity.

"Observers here for the Lutheran Church—Missouri Synod, the largest American Lutheran body outside the federation, said the discussion had shown that many who professed to be Lutherans were in serious need of re-indoctrination.

"The observers indicated that what they had heard so far seemed only to buttress their church's objections to joining the federation."

"The two official observers here for the Roman Catholic Church... said they felt the Catholic and Lutheran positions were slowly moving a little closer together."

The Australian Lutheran for September 18th, 1963, carried a report by Pastor Hans Lutz-Poetsch, an accredited press representative at Helsinki, who writes:

"Two things became evident from the whole procedure. First, that the member-churches of the Lutheran World Federation and their representatives are by no means any longer one in the central doctrine of the Christian and the Lutheran Church. Rather, 'a kaleidoscope of opinions' (as a leading representative of a German State Church expressed himself) became manifest to our shame. Secondly, what the former President of the World Federation said before the Press Conference in connection with the plenary session is revealing. A reporter asked him: 'Bishop, one could get the impression from the course of the second Vatican Council so far, that the progressives have had a victory over the traditionalists. Would one have to say now that it was the other way about in Helsinki?' Dr. Lilje answered: 'No! That you cannot say. I would prefer to say that the traditionalists were more in the shop-front.' The Bishop then continued to state that according to his opinion the plenary session had erred in rejecting the draft of the statement on justification. But the new Executive Committee would be in a position to make some changes in the personnel of the Commission on Theology. 'There are some amazing theologians in our Lutheran Churches, who busy themselves with modern theology,...'for instance the American, Nelson. And many a professor will be quite happy, if he can again give himself exclusively to his theological research and write books instead of having to attend sessions of the Commission. In other words—and the reaction of the press representatives clearly showed that it was thus understood and had to be understood in that way: 'Those who opposed the modern theology...which had found expression in the rejected document, would have to yield their places.' Time will tell whether such church-political manipulation will help a debated doctrine to establish itself within the Lutheran World Federation. A glance at the names of those who are on the new Executive of the Federation gives cause to hope that Bishop Lilje will meet with considerable opposition, if he thus seeks to attain his object."

Conclusion

Both Lutheran synods of Australia owe their very existence, humanly speaking, to the confessional obedience and courage of those God-fearing men and women, a hundred years ago, who left house and home for conscience' sake, because the established "Lutheranism" in Europe had become corrupt. Since then, the conditions that drove them out, have not improved materially. If anything, the territorial churches have sunk deeper into the corrosive acids of Rationalism. Neither Australian synod has any reason to re-embrace the apostasy which their forefathers renounced! God says: "avoid them" (Rom. 16:17); "Wherefore COME OUT FROM AMONG THEM" (II Cor. 6:17)! K. Marquart, Toowoomba, Dec. 13.

Christian News, December 30, 1963

1. Where are the clergy of the territorial churches of Europe trained? ____
2. What rule prevails at these universities? ____
3. What did Bultmann reject? ____
4. What is rationalism? ____
5. Rationalism did away with ____.
6. What did W. Oesch say about the theological complexion of Europe? ____
7. Gustaf Wingren said that Barth has the ability to ____.
8. To the contemporary thinker theological statements are statements containing ____ rather than ____ truth.
9. Gustaf Aulen insisted there is no such thing as ____.
10. Bultmann said that the Bible must be freed from ____.
11. Bishop Lilje hoped that ____ into the congregations.
12. What did Lilje say about Barth? ____
13. Who was Dr. Franklin Clark Fry? ____
14. What did Joseph Sittler deny? ____
15. *Conversation on Faith* of the LCA's Muhlenberg Press denied ____.
16. The trouble with Helsinki was ____.
17. What did H. Hamann Sr. show in the *Australasian Theological Review*? ____
18. What dangerous heresy did the official statement on Justification of the LWF Commission on Theology promote? ____
19. What is the pet notion of modern theology? ____
20. What seems to be taken for granted everywhere? ____
21. What does *simul justus et peccator* mean? ____
22. What did Bishop Bo Giertz attack? ____
23. Bishop Jacobi of Oldenburg said that to adopt the report would mean

to encourage ____.
24. The LWF was intensely wooing ____,
25. Would Bultmann have been welcomed at the LWF Assembly in Helsinki? ____
26. What did Han Lutz Poetsch report? ____
27. If anything, the territorial churches have sunk deeper into ____.

THE DOCTRINE OF JUSTIFICATION

By Prof. Kurt E. Marquart
Concordia Theological Seminary
Ft. Wayne, Indiana

*The following three lectures are the 1977 Reformation Lectures
which the author presented at Bethany Seminary, Mankato, MN*

LECTURE I
Justification Today

A. The Ecumenical Appearance
Warren Quanbeck has written:

1. "The doctrine of justification by faith was the subject of furious controversy in the 16th century. Theologians of both traditions can agree today because of the contribution of biblical and historical studies . . . Today biblically informed theologians in both traditions can agree on the teaching of the New Testament concerning justification by grace through faith, and can agree on theological formulations of the doctrine without denying or betraying their theological heritage. That this agreement is not known or acknowledged by every theologian and churchman in both traditions is not disproof of the statement but only testifies to the time lag between the work of specialists and more popular presentations."[1]

2. In other words, there is a Roman Catholic/Lutheran convergence today on justification. Out of the total material, we shall select two books in particular, commenting on certain issues raised there: (I) Hans Kueng, **Rechtfertigung** (1975) (2) Vinzenz Phnur, **Einig In Der Rechtfertigungs lehre?** (1970).

3. Kueng's famous book seeks to establish a basic harmony between Karl Barth and the Council of Trent on Justification. Since Barth consciously departs from Luther and the Reformation on this issue, the discussion is not directly relevant. Yet both Barth and Kueng make many very evangelical statements. And the Council of Trent is given a startlingly "evangelical" interpretation, or at least that is the impression. Yet Kueng approves very much of Cardinal Newman's Lectures on Justification, which are anti-Lutheran, though partly based on misunderstanding. Kueng, too, (p. 274 ff) is able to show that Barth is not alone but represents a general shift of Protestants away from pure juridical imputation to actual renewal as part of justification. Kueng expresses the doubt, however, whether the Reformation originally really taught the purely imputative view at all. His basic conclusion:

"The Protestants speak of declaring righteous, and the (Roman) Catholics of making righteous. But the Protestants speak of declaring righteous, which includes making righteous, and the (Roman)

27

Catholics of making righteous, which presupposes the declaring righteous" (p. 218).

4. Much more exciting, from a Lutheran point of view, is the painstaking dissertation by Pfnuer, also a Roman Catholic scholar. He limits his study to the justification controversy immediately surrounding the *Augsburg Confession* and the *Apology*, up to the year 1535. The point: both sides were largely fighting straw men. The Lutherans quite legitimately rejected the Pelagianising excrescences of the late, decadent stages of scholasticism, especially in its Scotist and Ockhamist forms, and especially as represented by Gabriel Biel, whose formulations, verbatim, are rejected in the *Apology*. But, says Pfnuer, by the time of 1530, none of the Roman theologians who opposed the Lutherans held to Biel's views or defended them. (Is not such a quick and dramatic change somewhat of a historical mystery, if true?) However, Eck and Company in turn were reacting not to Luther's and Melanchthon's mature formulations — say the Augustana and the *Apology* themselves, but to very early, unguarded, "extremist" statements, especially by Luther, long since left behind. Pfnuer presents an extremely sympathetic understanding of the Lutheran view, and since, on the Roman side, he is talking not about the Council of Trent but about the view of individual controversialists, he is able to deal with them more objectively and critically than Kueng was able to do in respect of the official, Tridentine definitions.

B. Analysis 1: Trent Revisited

5. What really were the specific points of difference over justification, and what stand did the Council of Trent actually take? My major resource here is the critical, though pro-Roman Catholic history of the Council by Hubert Jedin (*Geschichte des Konzils von Trient*), (available in English), of which 3 volumes have so far appeared (1951, 1957, 1970). Martin Chemnitz and Paul Sarpi are of course taken for granted. Jedin's history, however, is based on sources not formerly available.

6. The leaders of the Council were fully aware that, as the papal legates wrote to Rome on June 21, 1546, the article of justification was "the most important item before the Council" (Jedin, II, 144). But how to delineate the issues? Chemnitz saw very clearly that it was on the specific question of "the good works of the reborn" that "the chief controversy between us and the pontifical party" turned.[2] Are they or are they not wholly or in part the ground of our justification? If we now let Chemnitz speak more fully to this point we shall make the amazing discovery that he sounds as if he were replying quite specifically to the contentions of Newman, Kueng, and other moderns.

7. For all the Tridentine decrees concerning justification are so formulated that they indirectly accuse us as if we taught that the believers have only the forgiveness of sins, but that they are not also renewed by the Holy Spirit; also, that Christ earned for us only the reconciliation and not also at the same time the renewal, as if we excluded the renewal. Charity, or new obedience in such a way that it is neither present nor follows in the reconciled....

8. But someone may say: If matters stand thus, then what is it about which you contend so sharply concerning the article of justification, so that you throw almost the whole world into turmoil? Certainly, as you do not deny the renewal nor simply reject charity, so the papalists do not deny the remission of sins, but confess it. And if there is agreement about the matters themselves, there will then be only contentions about words or a war about grammar. For the papalists understand the word "justify" according to the manner of the Latin composition as meaning "to make righteous" through a donated or infused quality of inherent righteousness, from which works of righteousness proceed. The Lutherans, however, accept the word "justify" in the Hebrew manner of speaking; therefore they define justification as the absolution from sins, or the remission of sins, through imputation of the righteousness of Christ, through adoption and inheritance of eternal life, and that only for the sake of Christ, who is apprehended by faith. And yet they teach at the same time that renewal follows, that love and good works must be begun. Therefore there will be no contention about the matter itself, but only about the word "justification," which arises from this, that each understands and interprets that word differently. It is certainly not fitting in the church to cause disturbances about words when the matters themselves are safe . . . I Tim. 6:4 . . .

9. I have reported this objection in order that it might be possible to explain and show more readily and plainly what is the **krinomenon** ("point of difference"), or what is the true issue, of this controversy concerning the article of justification . . . We are by no means such troublemakers that we are so opposed to a true, solid, and salutary concord and so greedy for contentions . . .

10. For this is the chief question, this is the issue, the point of controversy, the **krinomenon**; namely, what that is on account of which God receives sinful man into grace; what must and can be set over against the judgment of God, that we may not be condemned according to the strict sentence of the Law; what faith must apprehend and bring forward, on what it must rely when it wants to deal with God, that it may receive the remission of sins; what intervenes, on account of which God is rendered appeased and propitious to the sinner who has merited wrath and eternal damnation; what the conscience should set up as the thing on account of which the adoption may be bestowed upon us, on what confidence can safely be reposed that we shall be accepted to life eternal, etc.; whether it is the satisfaction, obedience, and merit of the Son of God, the Mediator, or indeed, the renewal which has been begun in us, the love, and other virtues in us. Here is the point at issue in the controversy, which is so studiously and deceitfully concealed in the Tridentine decrees. This I wanted for once to explain simply yet more fully that the reader may see that what has been placed into controversy in this topic is not a strife about words but a very serious matter and uniquely necessary for consciences. And when all disputations about this topic are brought under this scope, then all things are plainer.[3]

11. There is no dispute about whether natural man, without grace, can

be justified before God by his works, or through the Law: this Pelagian view is rejected by Trent in the first three canons on Justification.[4] (cf. Council of Orange, 529, canons on grace, Denzinger, 176 ff.).

12. The Tridentine scheme of justification may be summed up like this: the sinner, his will freely co-operating with the promptings of divine grace, prepares himself turning to God. God then, normally through baptism, gives the free gift of justification. At this initial stage justification consists of the forgiveness of sins plus interior renewal, so that the person is not merely called righteous, by imputation, but actually is such, internally. This phase occurs without human merit, gratis, although free will is held to co-operate (synergism), and it is specially denied "that all works that are done before justification. In whatever manner they have been done, are truly sins of deserving of the hatred of God" (D, 817). But now there commences a second phase or stage of justification. The justified person, by virtue of Christ with His grace living in him, advances in holiness, good works, keeping the commandments, which have the effect of producing "the increase of justification" and "truly merit increase of grace, eternal life, and the attainment of that eternal life" (D, 803.842).

13. This amounts to the idea that Christ did not simply earn our salvation, but that he earned for us the chance to earn it — an assertion which distorts the Gospel beyond recognition. Of course it is denied in that scheme that salvation is obtained through faith alone. Paul's language to this effect is interpreted to mean simply that faith is "the foundation and root of all justification, 'without which it is impossible to please God' (Heb. 11:6)" (D, 801) — the very notion explicitly rejected in *Apology* IV, 71. For the "faith" envisioned at Trent is of itself purely intellectual and requires "love" to be effective or "formed". Hence: "If anyone shall say that justifying faith is nothing else than confidence in the divine mercy which remits sins for Christ's sake, or that it is this confidence alone by which we are justified: let him be anathema" (D, 822). Tridentine "faith" is not lost even when one falls from grace and justification, so that among those excluded from the kingdom of God are "also the faithful (!) who are 'fornicators, adulterers, effeminate, liers with mankind, thieves, covetous, drunkards, railers, extortioners' (I Cor. 6:9 ff)" (D. 808).

14. The whole scheme, and many of its particulars, are so inept and incongruous, that they give the impression of carelessness or unfamiliarity with the subject-matter. Kueng deplores Barth's opinion that "the concern of the Reformers didn't seem to make the slightest impression" on Trent (Rechtf., p. 110). Kueng replies that the document on justification took "seven months of intensive labor" to prepare, and that even the Lutheran, Rueckert, admits that the Council was concerned, in the matter of justification, exclusively with the problem of facing up to Luther, if so, the result is all the worse, although it represents undoubtedly a piece of church-diplomatic ingenuity.

15. In other words, the unevangelical merit-scheme of Trent was the result of a deliberate decision, not of oversight or misunderstanding. The most characteristic event here was perhaps the unambiguous rejection

of the notion of a two-fold righteousness, one imputed and one inherent.

16. Luther (LW, 31, 297 ff) and the *Formula of Concord* (III) speak of the perfect imputed righteousness of Christ by which we are saved, and the imperfect, inchoate righteousness in believers which necessarily flows from faith, but must not be regarded as meriting justification or eternal life. This two-fold righteousness was also agreed on, briefly, at the Regensburg Colloquy in 1541, in what must be regarded as a stunning coup on the part of the evangelically minded Cardinal Contarini.

17. At Trent it was Seripando, the General of the Augustinians, who led the fight for the recognition of a "double righteousness," though more in an Augustinian than a Lutheran sense. On October 15, 1546, the papal legates submitted to the Council theologians two questions, the first of which read:

"Has the justified person, who has, in the state of grace and with the help of divine grace, both of which come from the merit of Jesus Christ, done good works and thus preserved the inherent righteousness, satisfied the justice of God to the extent that he, placed before the judgment seat of Christ, receives eternal life on account of his merit — or does he need, besides the inherent righteousness, also the mercy and righteousness of Christ, that is the merit of his suffering, to supplement the defects of his own righteousness, though in such a way that this righteousness is communicated to him according to the measure of his faith and his love?" (J, II, 209-210) This was resolved into two sub-questions: "Does the possession of sanctifying grace satisfy the justice of God sufficiently to acquire merit and eternal life: Or does the person received into grace need beyond this still a divine act of grace which supplements, from the merit of Christ, the defects of the inherent righteousness?" (p. 213). Of the advisory theological experts, thirty definitely affirmed the first question and denied the second. Six gave the opposite answer, and one affirmed both subquestions! The Council voted accordingly. Seripando thought that "nearly all sought to exclude the righteousness of Christ from the hearts of men" (p. 219). When the justifying function of faith was limited to its preparatory role, Seripando wrote in the margin: "What do I hear? Everything written in Holy Scripture about justification by faith is to be understood of preparation?" (p. 239).

18. Lest there be any misunderstanding to the effect "that the righteousness of Christ is the formal cause or joint cause of justification, in place of or besides the inherent righteousness" (p. 238), formulations were brought forward which finally resulted in the present wording according to which "the unique formal cause" of justification is the inherent righteousness (D, 799). Canon 10 condemns those who say that the justified are "formally just" by Christ's "righteousness itself" (D, 820).

19. Such was "the answer of the ecclesiastical teaching office to Luther's and the Augsburg Confession's doctrine of grace and of justification" (J, 11, 260)! And despite self-contradictory attempts to adapt

Luther's "saint-and-sinner" concept, Kueng exclaims with Trent:

> God pronounces the verdict, 'You are just.' And the sinner is just, really and truly, outwardly and inwardly, wholly and completely (Justif. p. 213).
> It is to be presupposed that the justified man is **truly** just — inwardly in his heart . . . Justification is not merely an externally pasted-on 'as if'. Man is not only **called** just but he is just . . . not just partly but **totally**. . . (p. 236).

C. Analysis 2: Justification in Apology IV and FC III

20. The much-debated paragraph 72 of *Apology* IV explicitly distinguishes two senses of what it means to "be justified": (1) "to be made righteous out of unrighteous (persons) or to be regenerated"; (2) "to be pronounced or considered righteous (persons)". Nor is the *Apology* saying that one sense is right and the other wrong, or one proper and the other improper; on the contrary, the article itself adds: "Scripture speaks both ways."

21. The problem is that this appears at first sight to concede that Scripture sometimes uses the word "justification" to include also that inner renewal which we now call "sanctification". This would amount to a wider sense of the term to include not only justification itself, but also its effects, i.e., the new obedience. In any case, however, the *Apology* makes it crystal clear in many places that these effects, viz., the interior renovation, new obedience, good works, love, or sanctification, are in no sense the basis, ground or cause of acceptance before God, i.e., justification properly speaking.

22. According to this commonly held view, then, the *Apology* represents a broader understanding of justification, which was later, in the *Formula of Concord* (III) narrowed and flattened into the strictly forensic notion of imputation pure and simple. From this perspective, too, the *Formula*'s explanation of the *Apology*'s use of words like "regeneration" and "vivification" for "justification" (SD III, 18-20) must seem lame and labored, if not downright mistaken.

23. The solution to this entire problem, however, lies. I am convinced, in a different direction. The simple fact is that by "regeneration" or "the unrighteous being made righteous" the *Apology* in this context does not mean any effect or consequences of justification at all (such as love, good works, etc.). Rather, the *Apology* means simply the divine bestowal of faith itself, which alone makes alive because it alone can and does receive justification! The inner logic is: faith alone justifies, and faith itself is totally a Spirit-wrought gift. Since there can be no justification (subjectively!) without justifying faith, the gift or bestowal of that justifying faith must itself be a part of an aspect of justification. In other words, regeneration is equivalent to justification only because and to the extent that regeneration is the bestowal of justifying faith. Renewal in the sense of love and good works is not the meaning of regeneration here. Thus par. 72 concludes with the clearest possible equation: ". . . that faith alone

turns the unrighteous into the righteous man, that is, (hoc est), accepts the remission of sins." Parallel formulations like par. 76-78 confirm this understanding. Here the love and good works which follow from faith are clearly distinguished and excluded from justification, which happens *sola fide* (by faith alone) and means "to be made out of an unrighteous man a righteous one, or to be regenerated."[5]

24. The *Formula of Concord* is quite right therefore in saying that the *Apology* often uses the terms regeneration and vivification as equivalents of justification. But does not the *Formula* equate justification itself solely and alone with the forensic imputation, to the exclusion of all other aspects — also of the bestowal of faith? Not quite. Everything leading up to justifying faith (viz., contrition), and everything flowing from justifying faith (viz., love, good works) is excluded, but not faith itself (cf. SD III, 24-53). And while conversion and justification are distinguished, the *Formula* is careful to say not that conversion as such does not belong into the article of justification, but only that "not everything that belongs to conversion, belongs simultaneously also into the article of justification" (par. 25). The *Formula*'s very defense of the *Apology*'s use of "regeneration" and "vivification" for justification implies that the bestowal of faith itself is rightly regarded as part and parcel of justification. FC III specifically states: "For since man is justified through faith (which only the Holy Spirit works), this is truly transferred from death of life, as it is written: 'when we were dead in sins He has made us alive with Christ,' Eph. 2. Again: 'The righteous shall live by his faith,' Rom. 1" (par. 20).

25. It seems to me therefore that a statement like the following one by Poehlmann is wrong on two counts: "Whilst for the early Confessions justification is a declaring righteous and a making righteous at once, in the *Formula of Concord* it is understood purely forensically-imputatively, and sanctification is excised from justification and placed after it (nachgeordnet)."[6] In the first place, the *Apology* excludes sanctification from justification just as firmly as does the *Formula*. But secondly, neither the *Apology* nor the *Formula* are so "purely forensic" as to exclude the regenerating gift of justifying faith itself from justification. And the *Formula* insists just as strongly as does the *Apology* that sanctification (in the sense of love and good works) necessarily accompanies justification as its fruit and result.

26. Poehlmann's formulation, "Justification is acquittal and sanctification at once" misrepresents the biblical teaching of the Confessions. Also, it is difficult to see the logic of it. If Poehlmann dislikes the idea of a "purely forensic" imputation, his own formulation is nevertheless compelled to recognize this element; only he no longer calls it "justification," but substitutes the word "acquittal" (Gerechtsprechung). What is gained by this terminological juggling? One gathers that Poehlmann means to ward off the horrendous notion that justification is simply a sterile legal fiction, which leaves sinners as dead in trespasses and sins as they were before. This frightful caricature, however, was never the meaning and intent of the conscious stress on the forensic nature of justification, as it is found not only in the *Formula* and in Melanchthon, but above all in

Luther himself. Poehlmann's re-formulation, on the other hand, with its ambiguity about cause and effect, lends itself to an evasion of the central issue between Trent and the Reformation on justification, viz., whether sanctification (love, good works) gains or helps to gain God's acceptance, or whether it results from that acceptance.

27. Poehlmann, moreover, is not alone. The trend to mingle and confound faith and works, justification and sanctification. Law and Gospel, has become widespread and endemic in Protestantism.[8]

D. The Secular Reality

28. In a sense inter-church discussions of justification are — however horrible this may sound in Lutheran ears — an anachronism today. So many basic foundation-stones of Christian substance have crumbled for the reigning, historical-critical theology, that arguments about "justification" in that context are hollow formalities — rather like obligatory verbiage about "freedom, democracy, and human rights" in the mouths of Brezhnev and Idi Amin.

29. The Eastern Orthodox writer Konstantinos E. Papapetrou rightly sees the whole prevailing theological climate as a relentless secularization of Christian thought: "Today all of Christendom is being gradually, slowly but surely secularized. Even the Second Vatican Council seems in a certain respect to be the great Council of the secularization of the Roman Catholic Church..." [9] Neither Rome nor Lutheranism have remained untouched by the dead and deadening hand of the historical-critical devastation.

30. Consider the dramatic opening statements in a significant article by the *Los Angeles Times* religion writer John Dart (5 Sept. 1977): True or false?

— Jesus did not regard himself as God made flesh and probably did not call himself the Messiah.

— Jesus did not rise bodily from the dead. If you said "false", you are in step with popular understanding of the New Testament but out of step with the prevailing views of most prominent biblical scholars.

31. For Bultmann — whose heirs, disciples, and sympathizers infest all major Western church-bodies — doctrines like the Trinity, the Divinity of Christ, Incarnation, Redemption, Resurrection, and Ascension, were just so much myth and legend. Yet he continued to speak of justification, Law and Gospel, faith, and the like! But what can "justification" or even "faith" possibly mean without the divine-human Christ, His atonement and resurrection?

32. The plain fact is that at the official "ecumenical" level the supernatural substance of Christianity has virtually been replaced with various secular schemes of political and economic salvation! This social gospel dominates the Lutheran World Federation (Evian!) no less than the World Council of Churches. Where the Gospel is thought to include "world development," there "justification" can amount to little more than a thin veneer of bread-coloring on the lifeless stones of worldly, political

obsessions. Three random samples will have to suffice here. Poehlmann, who was cited above, states rather provocatively:

> The social-revolutionary movement of Reformation times, Anabaptism and Pietism were, with their stress on the deed-character of faith, a necessary critical corrective to the Reformation. This holds similarly for the political theology of the present (p. 207).

33. Michael Rogness' chapter on "Secular Ecumenism" in the volume. *The Gospel and Unity*, issued in 1971 by the Lutheran World Federation's Institute for Ecumenical Research in Strasbourg, accepted the new secularity quite uncritically:

> If the world were by nature a worthless, fallen vale of wickedness, and if God revealed his grace and imparted his Spirit exclusively through the ecclesiastical sacraments, and if the church were the group of redeemed whose task it was solely to convert worldly sinners into its circumference, then our old ways of thinking would still be appropriate — and like it or not, these are the presuppositions behind much, of the church's traditional mentality. If, however, we acknowledge that God is "in the world," then the relationship between church and world is altered radically and fundamentally from our usual pattern of thinking that only the church "brings God, Christ, and the Spirit" into the secular orders. If God is already present not only as the law-giving preserver of the social order . . . but is also working redemptively and graciously among men, then we shall have to do some serious reexamination (pp. 174-175).

34. Finally, the volume *The Church Emerging: A U.S. Lutheran Case Study* (Fortress, 1977) must be seen to be believed. Edited by John Reumann, the book contains four major essays by ALC and LCA theologians, written in connection with the Lutheran World Federation's global study of the nature and mission of the church. The secularist corrosion here is nearly total: one author sees ecology as the major challenge, to be met by the adoption of process philosophy. Another considers liberation from "sexism" (a perfectly silly word which if it is to have any sensible meaning at all should refer to the absurdly exaggerated status of sex in our culture). The third author advocates, in addition to the Bible, also "a certain authority in modern thought per se," i.e., a "dual authority of doctrine and modern thinking" (p. 150). The fourth writer thinks that the "so-called Third World realities are helping us define both the content and meanings of God's good news" (p. 187). This "good news" includes the crassest Marxist fantasies, e.g. that the Communist conquest of Vietnam was liberation (p. 232), and that Red China is an admirable model (pp. 220.247) while "Christians ought not be surprised by the radical analysis of the oppressive nature of the Western economic order in the world" (p. 216)!

35. Of course, one must continue to talk about "Christ," "the Word," justification," etc. But how? Two concluding quotations will illustrate the

technique:

> To be sure that word is always becoming enfleshed in the concreteness of personal and communal history...It is neither culturally limited to Bethlehem nor historically limited to Good Friday. It is an eschatological word for all places and all seasons. And the idolatries that absolutize past expressions of the reception of that word must give way...

> Nor is the church the exclusive agency of redemption in the world. That is amply demonstrated by the wider history of human communities which shows the capability of "secular" movements to effect liberation ... (pp. 126-127).

> (We are to) overcome our depoliticized, privatized and at most heretical captivity to justification wrongly understood, and become engaged as evangelical partners in a mission of liberation.... (p. 235).

36. Editor John Reumann, it is true, seems none too happily about some of this material and expresses several forthright criticism. But the very fact that such horrendous crudities constitute nowadays acceptable theological discourse speaks for itself.

37. In the 16th century battle about justification and Trinitarian and Christological foundations confessed in the great Ecumenical Creeds could be and were taken for granted as indisputable. Since the 18th century Enlightenment this is increasingly no longer the case. Theological discussion today cannot get beyond meaningless formalities unless it is clear from the outset whether the ABC's of Christianity are to be acknowledge unabridged, in their full biblical realism, or whether they may be reduced to infinitely flexible word games. Can there be any doubt about these things where the teachings of the Book of Concord are seriously believed and confessed?

Footnotes:

1. Vilmos Vajta, ed., *The Gospel and Unity* (Minneapolis: Augsburg, 1971), pp. 135-136.

2. Ed Preuss, ed., *Examen Concilii Tridentini per Martinum Chenmicium* (Berlin, 1861), p. 153.

3. Fred Kramer, tr. *Examination of the Council of Trent* by Martin Chemnitz, Part I (St. Louis: Concordia, 1971), pp. 465. 467-468.

4 Denzinger, *The Sources of Catholic Dogma* (St. Louis and London: Herder, 1957), 811-813.

5. Friedrich Loofs, who began the modern discussion of this question in 1884, shows that Melanchthon's *Apology* simply follows Luther in stressing regeneration as the bestowal of justifying faith and hence of justification itself. See F. Loofs, *Leitfaden zum Studium der Dogmengeschichte* (Halle, 1906), pp. 825-826, n. 16.

6. Horst Georg Poehlmann, *Abriss der Dogmatik* (Guetersloh, 1973), pp. 192-193.

7. *Ibid.*, p. 211.

8. Henry P. Hamann, *Justification by Faith in Modern Theology*, Grad-

uate Study Number II. St. Louis: School for Graduate Studies, (Concordia Seminary, 1957. Also, H. P. Hamann, "Sanctification — A Symbolical, Exegetical, Dogmatical, and Homiletical Study," *Lutheran Theological Journal*, vol. 10, no. 3 (December, 1976), pp. 85-96.

9. Konstantinos E. Papapetrou, "Ueber die anthropologischen Grenzen der Kirche," in W. Maurer, Karl H. Rengstorf, E. Sommerlath, and W. Zimmermann, eds., *Arbeiten zur Geschiehte und Theologie des Luthertums* (Hamburg: Lutherisches Verlagshaus, 1972) p. 133.

From the March, 1978 *Lutheran Synod Quarterly*, Bethany Lutheran Seminary, 734 Marsh Street, Mankato, Minnesota 56001. $4.00 per year.

Christian News, April 17, 1978

LECTURE II
Who and What is "Evangelical"?

38. Cardinal Newman, in his famous Lectures on Justification, repeatedly links the Lutheran doctrine of justification, which he caricatures and combats, with a low estimate of the Sacraments in general and of Holy Baptism in particular. [1] This false impression has prevailed today in the Anglo-Saxon world, so that a "low" view of the means of grace is generally thought to go hand in hand with an "evangelical" insistence on Justification by grace alone, whilst a "high," sacramental understanding of the alone-saving Gospel is felt to correspond to a Romanizing doctrine of justification. This is quite topsy-turvy. How ironic, how sad, that a full, rich, and worthy regard for the God-given reality of the evangel should now be decried as "unevangelical"! (In actual fact, as Dr. Tom Hardt has pointed out again, Luther's doctrine of the means of grace was actually stronger, more realistic, than the subtly spiritualizing theory of Thomas Aquinas! [2])

1. "Chief Article" versus Systematic Strait-Jacket

39. It is necessary at the outset to clarify in principle the place of the article of justification in the total Christian scheme of things. Many today imagine that justification is a kind of self-contained, self-sufficient principle which gives rise to all other articles of faith, so that everything is in principle reducible to justification; and that this is the distinctively "Lutheran" understanding of the Gospel. In the case of the means of grace this would mean that everything important about God's Word and Sacraments could be known already from the very nature of justification by grace, and that, conversely, particular points about the means of grace which do not necessarily follow from justification, should be regarded as matters of "interpretation" which should not disturb the unity of the church. This fallacy, based as it is on careless half-truths, is far more destructive than may appear on the surface. It implies in fact the total dissolution of biblical Christianity into a few bloodless abstractions or into what one observer has called "a nightmare of Swedenborgian correspondences"!

40. Although justification is the very chief article of the Christian faith, and is so understood in the Lutheran Confessions, this cardinal doctrine is not a speculative principle, from which other articles may then be derived by deduction or inference. Everything indeed is deeply connected and related to justification, as Luther points out in his Galatians commentary; but justification is not a reductionist minimum, for the sake of which other biblical doctrines may be sacrificed or compromised. Hardt has strongly and convincingly characterized Luther's attitude:

> In Zwingli's view this major point, faith's eating, about which the parties agree, makes bodily eating of the sacramental Body unneces-

38

sary: "When we now have the spiritual eating, what is the use of bodily eating?" Again and again Luther's opponents emphasized the fact that the Real Presence lacks systematic support in the doctrine of justification. However, Luther makes no attempt to produce any such "pious" explanation. Instead he summarizes his view in a monumental sentence... "EVERY ARTICLE OF FAITH IS IN ITSELF ITS OWN PRINCIPLE AND REQUIRES NO PROOF BY MEANS OF ANOTHER ONE." [3]

41. Werner Elert makes the same point about St. Paul himself: Those who claim that St. Paul invented the Sacrament, adapting a simple Jewish meal to the requirements of the Oriental mysteries, are refuted by the fact that Paul does not attempt to derive the Sacrament from any of his great themes, especially justification. If anything, an external Sacrament is, on the fact of it, inconvenient in the context of Paul's vehement argumentation against justification by external performances! Yet for Paul the Sacrament is a great "given", something he has received from the Lord Himself (I Cor. 11:23). It is a monolith which is simply "there" by divine fiat, and requires no systematic derivations or excuses.

42. The end-product of the reductionist corrosion may be seen in Bultmann, who insisted on "Law and Gospel" and "justification through faith alone" — but regarded the relevant historical facts and miracles as legends, and the dogmas (Trinity, Incarnation, Atonement, Sacraments) as so much ancient mythology! No wonder Sasse lamented "the transformation of the sola fide and the theologia crucia into a lifeless speculation in Lutheran circles"![4] Actually our Church's *Apology* long ago repudiated the reductionist understanding of "faith alone" as a kind of "Occam's razor": "We do not exclude the Word or the Sacraments, as the adversaries slanderously claim. For we have said above that faith is conceived from the Word, and we very much exalt the ministry of the Word" (IV, 74).

43. But as, on the one hand, justification is presented as an all-powerful principle whose self-unfolding sets up the various points of Christian doctrine, so on the other hand it is commonly denied that Luther's view of the centrality of justification is really the position of the New Testament. The Lutheran World Federation's Commission on Theology submitted to the 1963 Assembly at Helsinki a document, on **Justification**, which stated in part:

The Reformers believed that Justification is the theme that dominates the entire New Testament. We now recognize that Justification is indeed an image present in the earliest Christian tradition, but as one image among the many used to set forth the significance of God's deed in Jesus Christ....

Can we continue to assert that the article on Justification is the **articulus stantis aut cadentis ecclesiae**, when even in the earliest period of the church's life it was possible to proclaim the Gospel without reference to it? It is possible that insistence upon the centrality of Justification is an example of the way Controversy shapes and perhaps

39

44. No wonder the same booklet holds: "Justification by faith remains a difficult and obscure doctrine" (p. 7)!

45. Another example is provided by Paul Althaus' comparison between Paul and Luther. Althaus, by the way, who alleges certain conflicts between Paul and Luther, feels free to side now with Paul, now with Luther! For example, he holds that Paul did not teach Luther's idea of the need for daily repentance and forgiveness. On this score we "find only in Luther the full expression of the truth." On the other hand Althaus thinks that Paul was not talking about his Christian existence in Romans 7, but about his pre-Christian past. Luther's contrary conviction is rejected. [5]

46. H. G. Poehlmann, too, accuses the Reformation of assigning "to the doctrine of justification a cardinal rank which of course it does not have in the New Testament, and hardly even in Paul." [6]

47. Hans Kueng naturally echoes such sentiments, attempting to portray the Reformation doctrine as an exaggeration. (He notes in passing that for Calvin justification was not absolutely the centre.[7]). Of Paul, Kueng says: "In the captivity and pastoral letters justification certainly has not been forgotten, but who would maintain that it here still belonged to the keenly perceived central themes, and who would on that account blame Paul!" [8] But Luther too did not speak much about justification, say, at Marburg, 1529; nor did he use the word in his classic explanations of the Second and Third Articles! Was it therefore for him no longer a "central theme"?!

48. A basic misunderstanding is revealed in this bold formulation of Kueng's: "The doctrine of justification is not the central dogma of Christendom — this has always been catholic doctrine, and Barth there continues, against Luther, the best catholic tradition — the **central dogma** of Christendom is the Christ-mystery...[9]" But of course Luther never meant that justification was the center, to the exclusion of Christ. He insisted that all texts about good works must be understood "for Christ," not "against Christ". In other words, the notion of human merit, of earning eternal life, etc., violates precisely the central Christ-mystery, and not some abstract, isolated notion of "justification". Moreover, the New Testament everywhere stresses precisely the salvific, soteriological "point" of the Christ-mystery — not its bare ontology: St. John 1:14:17; Acts 4:12; I Cor. 2:2; Eph. 1:3-12; 3:1-21; Phil. 2:5-11; etc. Indeed, Kueng's own very fine stress on justification as first of all the objective acquittal of mankind in and by the death and resurrection of Jesus,[10] should have suggested to him the centrality at least of this objective justification in the New Testament. As for Luther, had he regarded a narrow, abstract justification, rather than the mystery of salvation in Jesus, as the real center of the Faith, he would have had to treat the Third Article as central and crucial. In fact, he assigns that preeminence to the Second Article, i.e. precisely to the "Christ-mystery" (*Large Catechism*, Second Article, par. 33)! And John Gerhard, whom Pieper quotes (*Dogmatics*, II,

57) calls "the mystery of Christ" the "metropolis of the heavenly doctrine."

49. Salvation in Christ alone, then, is the divinely given center, which illuminates — but does not eliminate! — all the manifold aspects of the full-orbed divine truth of Scripture; and all parts of biblical teaching cohere indissolubly with this central, "crucial" mystery.

2. An "Evangelical" Analysis of the New Pentecostalism in Relation to Justification.

50. For several years now a remarkable magazine, *Present Truth*, has been receiving wide circulation. The publication originated in Australia and is "dedicated to the restoration of New Testament Christianity in this generation." The publishers further describe themselves as a "group of Christian scholars and businessmen without denominational sponsorship who have united to uphold the objective gospel amid the present deluge of religious subjectivism." Against "the barren wilderness of groveling internalism," i.e. "The popular and frantic effort to find satisfaction in some sort of religious experience." Present Truth wishes to maintain "those great principles upon which the Reformation was founded — namely: **1. Sola gratia. . . 2. Sola Christo. . . 3. Sola Fid**e. . . **4. Sola Scriptura**..." (vol. 3, no. 1. Feb., 1974).

51. Most remarkable is the fact that this magazine concentrates almost exclusively on a vigorous defense of the Reformation's doctrine of justification. Although the editors are not Lutherans, their zeal on behalf of this central doctrine easily exceeds that of the Lutheran World Federation, as does their forthrightness. One is amazed at the many quotations not only from Luther, but also from Melanchthon, Chemnitz, and the like, and even from the *Formula of Concord*! A great deal of attention is devoted to a running critique of the New Pentecostalism, or the "Charismatic Movement". A Special issue (September — October, 1972) was devoted entirely to "Justification by Faith and The Charismatic Movement." One article states very pointedly:

> The central thesis of the Pentecostal movement is that the baptism, or infilling, of the Spirit is a definite second blessing which comes at a time subsequent to conversion. This Pentecostal thesis is a complete negation of the truth of justification by faith....
>
> 1. The Pentecostal idea of a post-conversion baptism of the Spirit implies that God's act of justification is not sufficient to bring the infilling of the Spirit. . . .
>
> 2. The Pentecostal teaching implies (and sometimes states explicitly) that the experience of being baptized in the Spirit is something greater and beyond the justification which comes by faith. . .
>
> 3. Pentecostalism presents an unfortunate dichotomy of receiving Christ and receiving the Holy Ghost....
>
> 4. Pentecostalism makes two different events of the baptism into Christ and into the Spirit.

52. Another illuminating piece, "Protestant Revivalism, Pentecostalism, and the Drift Back to Rome," shows the deep historical roots and connections of this baffling movement. Apart from the Anabaptists, Os-

iander, and the Pietists, the story really begins with John Wesley and the tremendous spiritual revolution he spearheaded, which likely saved Britain from the bloodbath of a political revolution like the French. A problem in Wesley's theology was the notion of a sudden "second blessing," after ordinary justification and sanctification. This "second blessing" allegedly removed from the believer the last vestiges of sin, so that he was now perfect, or "entirely sanctified." Wesley himself, it seems, was too great and humble a man to claim attainment of this "second blessing" for himself. But his followers, some of them, put the idea into practice to the point of fanaticism.

53. These ideas, combined with frontier-style revivalism, led to an even greater stress on religious experience, and on emotional crisis as proof of genuineness. The fanatical "second blessing" perfectionism caused such upheaval in the Methodist Church, that the "holiness movement" was forced out of the Methodist Church into a score of separate denominations by the end of the 19th century. Meanwhile, the idea of a "baptism of fire" had become popular among holiness people. (A "Fire-Baptized Holiness Church" was founded in Iowa in 1895). This "fire" was alleged to be a kind of "third blessing," after entire sanctification. It took the form of shouting, screaming, falling in trances, or speaking in "tongues". The publication, *Live Coals of Fire*, founded in 1899, spoke of "the blood that cleans us, the Holy Ghost that fills up, the fire that burns up, and the dynamite that blows up." Thus the way was paved for Pentecostalism, which was not long in coming. A perfectly logical outgrowth of these trends, the movement began with Charles Parham at Topeka, Kansas, in 1900. Pentecostalism was an off-shoot of the Holiness Movement, which in turn had grown out of Methodist revivalism. About 1960 this movement began a spectacular phase of infiltration and penetration into virtually all "mainline" denominations. The crucial idea, that of "Spirit Baptism" as an experience distinct from mere "water baptism," looks remarkably like a direct descendant of Wesley's "second blessing"!

54. This analysis seems on the whole quite sound, and the contrast between a church-life based on the objective fact of justification (Christ for us) and one built on alleged experiences of the Spirit in us, could not be greater.

55. It is interesting that even the Lutheran Charismatic Renewal Newletter cheerfully admits the historical roots and connections: The New Pentecostal ("Charismatic") and the old Pentecostal movements "are clearly differentiated, but no longer do the charismatic seem slightly embarrassed by the fact that much of their outlook. . .comes from the 'holy rollers' of a few decades ago. Rather, instead we find a refreshing search in Wesleyan, Holiness and Pentecostal sources for the appearance of today's renewal in mainline bodies" (June, 1976).

56. The question that needs to be asked now is this: Does the *Present Truth* analysis go far enough? I submit that it does not, for reasons which, I hope, shall become clear shortly.

3. The Full Gospel versus The "Evangelical" Truncation

57. Despite the frequent references to Luther and even the Lutheran Confessions, the basic orientation of Present Truth is unmistakably of the conservative "Reformed" variety, which represents a rather solid, traditionalist version of "evangelicalism." But does that really make a difference when confronting a common foe like Pentecostalism in its various forms? Cannot Calvinist and Lutheran conservatives form a pretty solid "united front" on this issue? Some, perhaps many, Lutherans seem to think so. One U.S. Lutheran pastor wrote the editor of Present Truth: "I have received every issue of Present Truth and rejoice in this publication more than in any other periodical I have ever received. God bless your continued efforts to speak His truth in a clear and denominationally unbiased way."

58. Let us begin by noting just two items, both from the Special Issue we have been considering. First, there is an article entitled, "By blood and by water," in which the "water" does not refer to Baptism. Secondly, and more seriously, one of three crucial questions, designed to separate Romanizing and Reformation concepts of justification, asks: "Do you believe that Christ as a divine Person can dwell in your heart?" The "Answer Key" explains: "Rome says 'Yes' and the Reformation says 'No'. Note: Christ as a Person dwells in heaven at the right hand of God. While we are home in the body, we are absent from the Lord (see 2 Cor. 5:6; Eccl. 5:2). He is present in His Word and by His Spirit, and this is how He dwells in our heart by faith. . ."

59. With this hyper-Calvinist denial of New Testament Christology it is impossible to make common cause, much as one must appreciate many other fine statements and insights. This startling cleavage over basic Christology must surely remind both parties that the difference is over the nature of the Gospel itself. Do we face in God's Word and Sacraments realism or symbolism, incarnational solidity or spiritualizing? Indeed, if Word and Sacraments are taken merely as outward signs of inner gifts given directly by the Spirit, without means, then what defense in principle is there against Pentecostalism? Is Pentecostalism simply an advanced stage of Calvinism, a predictable decay-product?

60. At its deepest level, it seems to me, Pentecostalism is a quest for religious assurance. The unbelievable theological bankruptcy of modern Christendom has created a great void, which is driving people into a private religiosity of direct and immediate religious satisfactions and validations. What could be more reassuring than one's own personal experience, a direct pipe-line to God? Hence the attraction of "tongues," healings, miracles, transcendental Meditation, and the plain old occult.

61. It is very instructive in this connection to see what the real religious function of the "tongues" or "Spirit-Baptism" experience is conceived to be. "Lutheran" Charismatic Larry Christenson, in his book. *The Charismatic Renewal Among Lutherans*, cites a number of typical "testimonies": A pastor had come to the end of his tether. Kneeling in desperation before the altar on a Saturday morning, he challenged God: "Either you are going to be real, or I am going to quit. You can have the whole

thing back — this church, my ministry, and me. I'm just going through the motions. . ." Suddenly a clear voice said: "The Gift is already yours; just reach out and take it." Now comes the Crucial paragraph:

Obediently I stretched my hands toward the altar, palms up. I opened my mouth, and strange babbling sounds rushed forth. Had I done it? Or was it the Spirit? Before I had time to wonder, all sorts of strange things began to happen. God came out of the shadows. 'He is real!' I thought, 'He is here! He loves me!'

For the first time in my life I really felt loved by God... 'God, where have you been all this time? . . . Give us this key, so that we can unlock you for the whole world (pp. 17-18).

62. A young married school teacher reports: "In the last few years God has become more real and personal to me than He ever was before. . .This relationship has come in a number of ways: the gifts of the Spirit, however, were undoubtedly the impetus" (p. 19). A pastor's wife writes: "At bible camp, when I was sixteen, Jesus Christ became a real person to me... The first time I ever heard anyone speak in tongues I knew immediately that this was the same Spirit which I had experienced fifteen years before . . . My reaction after that evening was mainly fear, fear of the thing itself — that God could be that real — but mostly fear of people. . . . Perhaps God knows that we need a sign again to give us power against the distractions and temptations of the world, and to keep us single-minded" (pp. 21-22).

63. A "life-long Lutheran" was as a teenager, "filled with the Holy Spirit. I'm sure of it because I had the evidence of the gift of tongues" (p. 24). Finally, here is the story of a Lutheran housewife in the hospital: "I have been a Lutheran all my life and considered myself a Christian, although my faith at times was at a low ebb. When I look back on those years, I certainly realize what a poor Christian I have been. . . One day in my hospital room I realized that I was praying in a new language. . . I felt a closeness to God that I had never before experienced. . . . The Bible became more meaningful to me. It was like a light had been turned on to give me better insight and understanding. God had, through the Holy Spirit, become a new reality to me" (pp. 24-25).

64. It seems obvious that searching, struggling Christians (Romans 7!), even afflicted pastors deeply conscious of their weakness and unworthiness, will find in these spiritual success stories a dazzling temptation to obtain the experiences of "tongues" as the great remedy and solution to all their problems. For the message is clear: people were baptized, absolved, confirmed, heard sermons, read the Bible, prayed, received the Sacrament — and not much happened. Then they spoke in "tongues", and everything began to happen. "Tongues" here has the nature and dignity of a super-sacrament which suddenly "makes God real to me." There is not the slightest hint in the New Testament that "tongues" are supposed to "make God real," or make one "feel forgiven." All this is part of a tragic, sometimes frenzied, quest for religious assurance in a Protestant reli-

giosity which has been robbed of objective means of grace.

65. Another "Lutheran" charismatic, Rodney Lensch, puts the whole thing even more crassly:

> I believe that the baptism in the Holy Spirit and the gifts of the Holy Spirit, in addition to the Word and Sacraments, are to empower and equip the church for her ministry of proclaiming the Gospel of Jesus Christ. To be perfectly frank, I didn't feel loved of God although intellectually I could say, "Yes, but God's Word says you are even if you don't feel it." But when the Holy Spirit flooded my soul with love, I felt it. There was no need to keep quoting Bible passages. The Holy Spirit was now ministering that love from within my heart and not just through my intellect.[11]

66. Indeed, Christenson says elsewhere: "Jesus links us to himself by this chain of three links: repentance and faith, water baptism, and the baptism with the Holy Spirit. These three links form a perfect unity, and the believer's relationship with Christ is incomplete until all three links have been forged on the anvil of personal experience"![12]

67. Where then must we look for the theological source of this remarkable exaltation of emotional experience? Where lies the problem which the appeal to emotion seeks to answer? The tracks for the present situation were set four hundred years ago. One of Luther's very central concerns had been to overcome the monstrous spiritual uncertainty (**monstrum incertitudinis**) of medieval, scholastic theology. Luther once again grounded and centered spiritual life in the utterly dependable, objective Gift of God in Jesus, that is, in the Cross and Resurrection. And how and where do we now, centuries later, find this Gift? In the utterly objective Gospel and Sacraments of Christ, which are not information (though they are that too) but powerful, Spirit-filled, life-creating means of grace. Here forgiveness, assurance, life and salvation, indeed the whole treasury of heaven is effectively given and distributed to us by God, the Holy Trinity.

68. John Calvin, however, radically undercut this evangelical scheme. He taught the unbiblical notion of "double predestination": God does not seriously wish the salvation of all, but has from eternity predestined some to salvation and others to damnation. With rigid logic Calvin pursues the philosophical notion that whatever God wills must of necessity happen. [13] Hence damnation must be seen as being due not to the fault of man but to the decision of God![14] So inexorable is this logic that God's will not only "barred the door of life" to the non-elect but even "predestined the fall into sin"! [15]

69. This position is a disaster the magnitude of which can hardly be over-estimated. For as soon as the universality of God's serious, saving will in Christ is denied, no objective, reliable grounds remain for any assurance of salvation. It is said that Luther was once asked whether John 3:16 would not read even better if it said "God so loved Martin Luther..." instead of "the world." "Heaven forbid," Luther shot back, "then I would

always have to wonder whether there was another Martin Luther in the world!" It is precisely the universality of grace, the sacrifice of the Lamb of God for the sins of the world which is the absolutely indispensable basis of certainty. Calvin himself realized that in his scheme the Gospel itself could no longer in and of itself be the ground of faith: "because such preaching is shared also with the wicked, it cannot of itself be a full proof of election."[16] Actually this is quite an understatement. If Christ redeemed only part of mankind, and if forgiveness and salvation are offered by God only to some men, but not to others, then the Gospel and Sacraments become totally ambiguous and useless as grounds of faith, for in some cases God means it when He says "shed for you for the remission of sins," while in other cases He simply does not mean it, even though the very same words are used! Here is an uncertainty more monstrous than any medieval scholasticism! The real stress now cannot be on the objective Gospel and Sacraments, which have been demoted to neutral, noncommittal "signs," but falls on that inner "illumination" by the Spirit which can alone supply spiritual life and power, but which works in sovereign predestinational independence of the outward Word.[17] Despite Calvin's bravado about the continued importance of the outward Word, it is clear that this Word is really nothing, and the inner Spirit-action everything:

> Therefore I make such a division between Spirit and Sacraments that the power to act rests with the former, and the ministry alone is left to the latter — a ministry empty and trifling, apart from the action of the Spirit, but charged with great effect when the Spirit works within and manifests his power. [18]
>
> Yet since we see that not all indiscriminately embrace that communion with Christ which is offered through the gospel, reason itself teaches us to climb higher (!!!) and to examine into the secret energy of the Spirit, by which we come to enjoy Christ and all his benefits. [19]

70. But if the decisive thing is not the Gospel itself but an inner Spirit-action alongside it, then, in practical terms, this inner action can be identified and gauged only in the form of feelings, that is, emotional experience, it matters terribly that the elect "feel the working of the gospel,"[20] for the necessary confidence "cannot happen without our truly feeling its sweetness and experiencing it in ourselves." [21] To assign to feelings so central and decisive a role is to invite the direct mischief. The rise of something like Pentecostalism becomes then virtually inevitable, given favorable historical circumstances. For if the prize goes to inner experiences, then "tongues" are more dramatic and more tangible emotional indicators than vaguer, more ambiguous feelings. Moreover, once the "charismatic" spirit has gained a foothold, it will hardly be exorcised with paler, weaker forms of direct Spirit experience!

71. Theoretically therefore it would seem that Calvinism as such cannot provide any really firm defenses against Pentecostalism. Where it seems to do so, it is involved in a fundamental inconsistency. The *Present*

Truth group, for example, have provided absolutely magnificent materials which counter Pentecostal subjectivism as a religious basis with the utterly objective fact and gift of the Christ for us. But can this position really be maintained in practice without an equally objective doctrine of Christ's Gospel and Sacraments as means of grace? Is not an objective Gospel simply the expression of the objective Christ for us HERE AND NOW? If Christ is objective only then and there — two thousand years ago — but is here and now available only in inner Spirit — experience, has subjectivism really been challenged at all?

72. One notices the same dilemma in Francis Schaeffer's book *True Spirituality*. For all of Schaeffer's absolutely magnificent crusading against modern subjectivism and religious and philosophical experientialism, the book on spirituality seems utterly unable to point out objective elements strong enough to serve as bases and sources of spiritual life. Although one or two baptismal texts from the New Testament are cited repeatedly, there is no discussion of Baptism, of Holy Communion, or even of the effective spiritual power of the Gospel itself! How is it possible to write about true spirituality, in the context of the rabid modern experience cult, without at all discussing the only possible remedy? Instead there is much talk about "moment-by-moment" consciousness or awareness of "the supernatural" (why such horridly vague, theosophical-sounding language?) — in other words of basically mental activities. Christ did His work then and there, so that what is left to us is to think, remember, and meditate thereon by way of present inspiration and motivation. What is missing is the actual, live encounter, here and now, with the Person and Work of the Savior, not simply through the Spirit as "agent" for the (absent?) Trinity, but through objective Gospel-means throbbing with supernatural life and blessing from the ever-present Holy Trinity. Reminders, remembrances, and mental meditations are poor substitutes for the blessed reality. The church then becomes mainly a moral obligation, rather than a salvatory necessity and celebration.

73. What is merely tragic in Calvinism is inexcusable in Lutheranism. Yet the fact of the matter is that many of our people, while Lutheran in theory, are Calvinists in practice. That is, they view the means of grace and the church through the "spiritualizing" spectacles of the myriad Reformed paperbacks they have absorbed. How else can we explain the fact that the Living Bible has become immensely popular even among Lutherans, who do not seem to be bothered at all by horrid mutilations like these "translations" of Col. 2:12 and 1 Cor. 10:16:

> For in baptism you see how your old, evil died with him and was buried... When we ask the Lord's blessing upon our drinking from the cup of wine at the Lord's Table, this means, doesn't it, that all who drink it are sharing together the blessing of Christ's blood? And when we break off pieces of the bread from the loaf to eat there together, this shows that we are sharing together in the benefits of his body.

74. The reductionist, corrosive mood of our religious environment demands that we re-appropriate and maintain without compromise the New Testament fulness of the alone justifying Christ for us — not only

"then and there" but also "here and now" in the blessed means of grace. The effective ground and evidence of our confidence in Christ's justification must be the divine dynamic of the Gospel itself, not our own inner musings (cf. Rom. 1:16; 10:17; 1 Cor. 4:15; 15:2; Luke 8:11; Jn. 6:63). This salvatory dynamic, moreover, includes also the Gospel-actions, Baptism (Acts 2:38; 22:16; Rom. 6:4; Gal. 3:26-27; Eph. 5:26; Tit. 3:5; 1 Peter 3:21, etc.) and the actual "participation in the holy things" of Christ's body and blood, 1 Cor. 10:16 ff.

75. Where the full New Testament glory of the alone-saving Christ-mystery is thus worshiped in humble, childlike faith, there and there alone can the monstrous uncertainties of all subjective will-o-the-wisps be effectively resisted. Here is the objective and self-communicating Ground of our justification and salvation. Whoever has grasped this Pearl of great price will not hanker after glass trinkets!

Footnotes

1. John Henry Newman, *Lectures on the Doctrine of Justification* (Westminster, Md: Christian Classics, 1966), pp. 4,361.

2. Tom G. A. Hardt, *On the Sacrament of the Altar*. Typed manuscript in the possession of the Concordia Theological Seminary Library, Ft. Wayne, pp. 17-21.

3. *Ibid*, pp. 5-6.

4. H. Sasse, "The Crisis of the Christian Ministry", *Lutheran Theological Journal*, vol. 2, no. 1 (May, 1968), p. 44.

5. Paul Althaus, *Paulus und Luther* (Guetersloh, 1958), pp. 55, 77, 95.

6. Poehlmann, *op. cit.*, p. 192.

7. Hans Kueng, *Rechtfertigung* (1957), p. 25.

8. *Ibid.*, p. 213.

9. *Ibid.*, p. 128.

11. Rodney Lensch, *My Personal Pentecost* (Kirkwood, Mo.: Impact Books, 1972), pp. 42, 11.

12. Larry Christenson, *Speaking in Tongues*, p. 51.

13. John T. McNeill, ed.. *The Library of Christian Classics*, Vol. XXI. Calvin: Institutes of the Christian Religion (Philadelphia: Westminster, 1967), Book III, ch. XXIII 2, 8 (pp. 949, 956-7).

14. *Ibid.*, pp. 946-947, 956-957

15. *Ibid.*, pp. 931, 955.

16. *Ibid.*, p. 965.

17. *Ibid.*, pp. 538, 985, 1284-1294.

18. *Ibid.*, p. 1284.

19. *Ibid.*, p. 537.

20. *Ibid.*, p. 985.

21. *Ibid.*, p. 561.

Christian News, May 1, 1978

LECTURE III

Justification Versus "Cheap Grace"

76. Let us hear the scathing eloquence of Bonhoeffer:

We Lutherans have gathered like eagles round the carcass of cheap grace, and there we have drunk of the poison, which has killed the life of following Christ, it is true, of course, that we have paid the doctrine of pure grace divine honors unparalleled in Christendom... Everywhere Luther's *formula* has been repeated, but its truth perverted into self-deception. So long as our Church holds the correct doctrine of justification, there is no doubt whatever that she is a justified Church! So they said, thinking that we must vindicate our Lutheran heritage by making this grace available on the cheapest and easiest terms. To be "Lutheran" must mean that we leave the following of Christ to legalists, Calvinists and enthusiasts — and all this for the sake of grace. We justified the world, and condemned as heretics those who tried to follow Christ. The result was that a nation became Christian and Lutheran, but at the cost of true discipleship....

We gave away the word and sacraments wholesale, we baptized, confirmed, and absolved a whole nation unasked and without condition... We poured forth unending streams of grace. But the call to follow Jesus in the narrow way was hardly ever heard. . . . what had happened to all those warnings of Luther's against preaching the gospel in such a manner as to make men rest secure in their ungodly living? . . . What are those three thousand Saxons put to death by Charlemagne compared with the millions of spiritual corpses in our country today?... Cheap grace has turned out to be utterly merciless to our Evangelical Church (*The Cost of Discipleship*, SCM, London, 1959, pp. 44-45).

77. One may say that Bonhoeffer exaggerates, that his own theology was heretical, that he was speaking of conditions in secularized state-churches, and the like. And no doubt, it is true that, like Kierkegaard before him, Bonhoeffer blames Lutheranism for views and attitudes conditioned in fact by post-Enlightenment frauds and devastation. The pre-World War I "Christian, humanitarian and liberal tradition" in which Bonhoeffer grew up (*Discipleship*, p. 9) was heavily tinged with the optimistic ideology of A. Ritschl, whose denial of divine wrath, justice, and atonement in effect reduced God's love to mere sentimentality! Yet when all is said and done, the fact remains that there is terrible truth in Bonhoeffer's words, also for our contemporary, orthodox Lutheran congregations, it is perfectly true that "salvation by grace" is widely misunderstood as a license to take things easy spiritually, as a dispensation from holy living. We suffer from a widespread decline in moral seriousness, so that in place of an all consuming hungering and thirsting

after righteousness we often find a pathological loss of appetite.

It is futile and absurd to be forever and one-sidedly imploring crowds of comfortable modern people not to attempt to earn heaven by good works — when they really haven't the slightest intention of complicating or inconveniencing their lives with any serious interest in good works at all!

78. What is crucial here, of course, is the proper distinction between Law and Gospel. It is this right distinction and application alone, which makes all the difference between the life-giving administration of the central mystery of our holy Faith, and the death-dealing poisoning of Bonhoeffer's Lutheran vultures with the cheap grace of "justification by faith" as an embalmed intellectual abstraction. For only the proper distribution of Law and Gospel — that high and awesome art of which in this life we remain but humble apprentices — can achieve the divine objective of comforting the afflicted and afflicting the comfortable, rather than vice versa (see the *Magnificent* and all parallels)!

79. The observations, which follow, are not meant to be in any sense exhaustive. Nor are they but a collection of random thoughts. The intention rather is to high-light certain aspects of Law-proclamation on the one hand and of Gospel-celebration on the other; namely, those which seem at least to the present writer to require special emphasis today, in view of the cultural context in which our congregations must live and work.

I. Sin and Need

80. One of the prime deficiencies of our underprivileged age is an almost total absence of a sense of sin. Luther's "terrors of conscience" and his quest "for a gracious God" are perceived today, patronizingly, as something scarcely comprehensible, something from another and strangely antiquated world. The "modern" instinct is to assign the problem to the level of chemo- or psycho- therapy for guilt-feelings!

81. There are no doubt many reasons for the virtual evaporation of the notion of sin from the public mind. One of the chief factors must be the almost universal acceptance of the evolutionary view of man's origins. Our whole secular culture is built on this cultural myth, reinforced daily in a thousand subtle ways. Christians too must daily breathe this evolutionary atmosphere, which is bound to color their conscious and subconscious perception of reality.

82. The hideous moral relativism and nihilism issuing from this Godless view of the universe are daily becoming more explicit. From Freud to Kinsey to Ann Landers, from Elvis Presley to the latest TV starlet exuding oracular if inarticulate moral maxims for the masses, the message is predictable and in essentials unvarying: whatever is, is right; everything is beautiful in its own way; do your own thing; if it feels good, do it; guilt-feelings are pointless and old-fashioned, etc. *usque ad nauseam*.

83. The terrible thing about this decomposition of standards and behavior is that it is perfectly logical—given the worldview of our media-culture's pacesetters. If there is no God, then, as Nietzsche and

Dostoyevsky foresaw with crystal clarity, though from opposite poles, "anything goes." If there was no divine creation, then we are but freaks of nature, and our lives devoid of moral significance. Whether it be human life or a litter of puppies, spiders, worms, desert cactus or blades of grass, or indeed the deadly sterile surface of the moon, or even helium, hydrogen, atoms, molecules, and subatomic particles or energy vibrations: it is all the same to an empty universe rushing headlong into cosmic perdition and extinction! In such an absurd universe, moral values are but a trick of nature, a cruel joke. Apart from an eternal Creator and Judge, good and evil can mean no more than taste or preference, like liking or disliking oysters. Killing six million Jews might then still be emotionally distressing to most people, but intellectually it can mean no more than an unusual taste, an "alternative lifestyle"!

84. Few people have faced the de-humanizing implications of modern "humanism" more clear-headedly than the humanist Bertrand Russell, who wrote:

> That Man is the product of causes which had no prevision of the end they were achieving; that his origin, his growth, his hopes and fears, his loves and his beliefs, are but the outcome of accidental collocations of atoms; that no fire, no heroism, no intensity of thought and feeling, can preserve an individual life beyond the grave; that all the labor of the ages, all the devotion, all the inspiration, all the noonday brightness of human genius, are destined to extinction in the vast death of the solar system, and that the whole temple of man's achievement must inevitably be buried beneath the debris of a universe in ruins — all these things, if not quite beyond dispute, are yet so nearly certain, that no philosophy which rejects them can hope to stand. Only within the scaffolding of these truths, only on the firm foundation of unyielding despair, can the soul's habitation henceforth be safely built.[1]

85. H. J. Blackham, director of the British Humanist Association, quoted this remarkable passage in his essay, "The Pointlessness of It All," and commented: "It is too true to be good: let us acknowledge the truth, and provide the goodness ourselves, with pride and without hope."[2]

86. It should not be thought, however, that this philosophy affects only intellectuals, leaving the ordinary people unscathed. Frances Schaeffer has shown, especially in his splendid book, *The God Who Is There*, how this philosophy of meaninglessness has, through popular culture, engulfed the broad masses like a vast tide of pollution:

> *The Silence* is a series of snapshots with immoral and pornographic themes. The camera just takes them without any comment. "Click, click, click, cut!" That is all there is. Life is like that: unrelated, having no meaning as well as no morals....
> The posters advertising Antonioni's Blow-Up in the London Underground were inescapable as they told the message of that film: "Murder without guilt; Love without meaning."[3]

87. Most people will regard self-indulgence as the only sensible response to such an obscene universe. And that indeed is the basic thrust of much contemporary literature and drama. This point is well made in Professor Duncan Williams' book, *Trousered Apes*, sub-titled: "Sick literature in a sick society." The secret of happiness, we are told in this sick literature, lies in the satisfaction of our biological, organismic instincts and urges. Reason, morality, religion, culture, and the like, only get in the way, being artificial and therefore "hypo-critical" constructs. Malcolm Muggeridge put it well when he described Williams' book as "a cogently argued, highly intelligent and devastatingly effective anatomization of what passes for culture today, showing that it is nihilistic in purpose, ethically and spiritually vacuous, and Gadarene in destination"!

88. The tragedy is that the churches have yielded almost completely to these secular superstitions — hence, e.g., the jargon about avoiding anything "judgmental." Popular sloganeering makes the word "evangelical" mean about the same as "permissive." And in the name of this fraudulent pseudo-gospel people are being robbed of all clear moral categories, whilst their religion decays into a few self-serving clichés, like, "we're all sinners anyway." Here "sin" is no longer a horror but a comfort, almost a point of pride rather than a source of shame.

89. This deep corrosion cannot be reversed with touching rhapsodies about "the love of God" and tremulous verbiage about "the Cross" without an honest confrontation and unmasking of evil for what it is. It is just such pietistic evasions, which spawn unspeakable offenses like "Lutheran" abortionists, who sigh religiously about "evangelical freedom" and "responsibility" while they butcher helpless unborn babies for profit! Such moral cretinism, sad to say, appears to be more common among Lutherans than among Roman Catholics, who, whatever else may need to be said about their theology, are generally equipped at least with some basic and clear-cut moral categories!

90. But, our cheap-grace advocate may object, is not all this rather external, on the level of civic righteousness, hence far inferior to the real, spiritual righteousness of the Gospel? I can only reply that any "spiritual" righteousness, which is indifferent to the murder of human beings, is a sham and a fraud. The Lord says not that our righteousness is to be less than that of the scribes and Pharisees, but that it is to be more! The divine love of sanctification, to be sure, far surpasses the mere justice of civic righteousness. But a "love" being less than justice while purporting to be more, would not be love.

91. It sounds very pious to condemn all moral distinctions and categories as so much Talmudic, rabbinical legalism. "One sign is as bad as another — and didn't Christ Himself abolish casuistry?" No, the Lord did not abolish all distinctions. He clearly taught that some things are much worse than others and will result in different measures of punishment (Mat. 12:45; 21:28-32; Lk. 10:12-15). What He condemned was the invention and exploitation of self-serving distinctions (Mt. 23:16-22)! But the rejection of distinctions can be just as self-serving. When the Lord said that giving oneself to evil lust was as bad as doing the evil deed. He could

count on His hearers recoiling in horror from the evil deed. He was stressing the guilt of the thought, not the innocence of the act, the importance of the former, not the unimportance of the latter. In today's climate, however, people are likely to draw the opposite conclusion: not that thoughts are as wicked as deeds, but that deeds are as harmless as thoughts! In other words, if I am already "guilty" for thinking the evil, I may as well have the satisfaction of doing it as well. Here the denial of moral distinctions has become self-serving and productive of moral chaos.

92. A related excuse for moral laxity in the name of "cheap grace" is what we might call the fallacy of motivational perfectionism. It is the fallacy of the man who never gave more than 50 cents because, as he explained, the Lord loves a cheerful giver, and he simply couldn't be cheerful if he gave anymore! The inner logic of this fallacy runs something like this: human acts are worthless morally unless they are done for the right reason, from right motives, which must include sincerity. Therefore if I "don't feel like" doing something, I shouldn't do it, because I would not be "sincere" if I did. And so we neglect important Christian duties and functions, prayer, devotions, church, sacrament, help and service to our neighbor, while piously waiting for a spirit of sincerity and proper disposition to waft gently into our hands! But the whole point of Christian life, discipleship, and discipline is precisely to keep on doing what we, or rather our flesh, does not feel like doing! The spirit is always willing, but it dare never wait for the flesh — that will be weak until doomsday. The new man must daily arise, take up his cross, manfully crucify the flesh with its "feelings" and lusts, and assert anew the victory of Christ over the dragons of the world, the flesh, and the devil. To shirk duty and service for the uncertain prospect of fickle moods and feelings is to fall prey to one of the prime seductions of "cheap grace."

93. This wishy-washy sort of self-indulgence has a vested interest in moral muddle-headedness. Basically, the muddle reflects secular confusions and resists clarification. Here it is essential to preserve and assert the indissoluble connection between the First and Second Articles of the Creed. While it is true that the First Article is not properly believed except "through" the Second Article, it is also true, paradoxically, that the Second presupposes the First and collapses into vacuous sentimentality without it. Secular, evolutionary superstitions need to be thoroughly exterminated by means of a serious, credible doctrine of the Creation and Fall, without which the Redemption itself loses its point and savor. It is only within the framework of a realistic, no-nonsense reading of the First Article, that the Law can be treated with any sort of ultimate respect. Where Darwin and Freud are regarded as the real authorities on man's origin and nature, rather than Moses and Jesus, there the Law will never be more than a harmless, toothless old hound, to be endured with impatience perhaps, but certainly not with terror. Sin is sin only where God is God — hence the church's teaching and preaching must relentlessly and uncompromisingly break down all the secular idolatries that paralyze Christian minds, in order to release the latter into the glorious liberty of the children of God!

94. There is one more secular factor that needs to be considered in this context, and that is the prevailing success-and-achievement cult. This too cannot but have the effect of suppressing any serious consciousness of sin, for as Lefferts E. Loetscher observed laconically: "Men could not forever bow as wretched sinners on Sunday and swell with self-importance the other six days of the week"! The popularity among Lutherans of Norman Vincent Peale's crass promotion of success and self-confidence is an alarming index of the erosion of the Christian understanding of man and of life. The insatiable appetite, also among our people, for such "how to" books, offering themselves in the guise of practical, down-to-earth advice for the practice of Christianity in daily life, may also indicate a deficiency in the church's preaching and teaching in this regard. Mere theological generalities are not enough. People need concrete and continuous illumination, from the Word of God, of the relation between Christian piety and discipleship, and the problems and realities of daily life. If such guidance is not forthcoming from Lutheran pulpits and Bible classes, it will be so tight in a proliferation of courses and "institutes" which owing to their Calvinistic, legalistic, or even secularistic orientation, dangerously short-circuit the real evangelical and churchly source and basis of sanctification.

95. The impact of the secular success-cult has this in common with the New Pentecostalism's "Quest for Power," [5] that it entices the Christian away from Gethsemane ("not my will but Thine be done") and into the orbit of magic, which seeks to work one's own will on God and His world. This attitude regards the problems of sin as an initial, primitive stage of the Christian life, which is soon settled, and from which one then advances to "greater things," i.e., the preoccupation with "results," — especially gaudy fireworks like "healings" and "tongues." Genuine Christian growth by contrast is never finished with the problem of sin, retains lifelong an attitude of humble, ever-deepening penitence, and cultivates the resignation of Lazarus (St. Luke 16:19 ff.), and therefore quite deliberately finds joy and fulfillment not in earthly shadows but in the central miracle of Christianity; the love and mercy of God in His Son, freely and generously offered in His Word and Sacraments!

96. These means of grace become boring and "repetitious" only where the secular indifference to the frightful reality of sin has taken hold. From this insensitivity and boredom arises the dreadful demand that worship be replaced with some form of religious entertainment. And so the historic Liturgy, which for centuries has carried the precious communications between God and His people, is pushed out more and more, in favor of some saccharine "format" patterned after the inane banalities of television! Where is the consciousness of sin, or minimal respect for God, when the Christian mysteries are reduced — as happens regularly in some, perhaps many, Lutheran schools! — to a series of vulgar and raucous nightclub acts on religious themes, to the accompaniment of thumping, clapping, and guffaws from the audience? Truly, a proper understanding of the radical nature of sin is beyond the grasp of man's reason — it needs to be learned and inculcated again and again from God's

own Word (Apol. II, 13; IV, 164).

97. So far we have looked at the more external, environmental factors, which today conspire to create a climate deeply hostile to the very idea of sin. But is there something in the Lutheran doctrine of justification itself which is one-sided, distorted, and therefore bound to work itself out in history as "cheap grace"? Is Lutheranism a balanced, integrated version of biblical Christianity, or is it simply a protest, a reaction, incapable of an independent, positive existence (e.g., last century's "Anti-Missourian Brotherhood"!)?

98. Luther himself was fully aware of the horrendous potential for evil which lay in the abuse of his doctrine. Indeed, he had a good taste of it during his own life-time already. The *Large Catechism*, for instance, refers repeatedly to the "swinish," "loutish" behavior of those who misunderstood and misused the new freedom of the Gospel to embrace total Epicurean abandon. Such people, writes Luther in a brief appendix on Confession, have no idea what the Gospel is. They deserve to be returned to the pope's tyranny, to be driven, compelled, and tormented harder than ever before! "For the rabble who refuse to obey the Gospel are fit for nothing but such a torturer, to be God's devil and hangman!" (par. 6)

99. Actually the objection that his doctrine encouraged moral laxity and dissipation was not new; it had been urged already against St. Paul (Rom. 3:8; 6:14,15) and, by implication, against the Lord Himself (St. Matthew 11:19). But like the Lord and St. Paul, Luther refused to "save" the Gospel by adulterating it with moralizing "safeguards". Such a cure would have been worse than the disease — seeking to prevent the abuse of the Gift by abolishing the Gift! Yet no one can accuse Luther of not stressing the necessary consequences of faith and justification. The *Large Catechism's* explanation of the Ten Commandments is in large measure the so-called "third use of the Law."

100. And the Creed is regarded as "enabling us to do what according to the Ten Commandments we must do" (par. 2). From a true, evangelical knowledge of God "we get pleasure and love towards all the Commandments of God, because we see here how God gives Himself to us wholly and entirely with everything that He owns and can do, as Help and Support for us, to keep the Ten Commandments" (par. 68-69). Here in this life of course we "remain half and half pure and holy, so that the Holy Ghost may ever work in us through the Word and daily distribute forgiveness until that life where there will be no more forgiveness, but completely and entirely pure and holy people, full of piety and righteousness, liberated and free from sin, death and all misery in a new immortal and glorified body" (par. 58).

101. No, it is not from Luther that modern Lutherans have learned the Pharisaism of the publican: "God, I thank Thee, that I am not as other men are, scrupulous, self-righteous, moralists, or even as this Pharisee. I never fast, but commit adultery twice a week, and am not so superstitious as to pay conscience-money to the church!"... Whose damnation is just, as St. Paul observes, Rom. 3:8.

102. All good gifts of God — above all His greatest and best: His own

forgiving grace — are meant for our welfare and salvation. And all of them can be abused quite contrary to the divine intention. The fault lies not in His good gifts, but in our wicked flesh, which seeks to twist and manipulate everything to its own self-seeking, idolatrous ends. As for justification, the mere verbal *formula* can be got right by saint or scoundrel alike: what is all-important is the right application, it is one thing to offer Gospel-consolations to the tormented Christian who seeks earnestly to keep the Commandments and finds that he cannot; it is quite another to cast these pearls before hedonistic swine who seek from religion only a cloak of respectability for continuing exactly as they are. Or, to use Kierkegaard's example: when a wise old scholar, after a lifetime of strenuous intellectual labor, confesses that "we can know nothing," he utters a noble truth. The young student expressing the same sentiment to excuse his own laziness is but mouthing a phrase, without integrity. Just so the Lord offers rest to those who "work hard and are heavily burdened," viz., under the conviction of God's holy Law, but not to those who couldn't care less!

103. Finally, if the devil can't get to us in one way, he will try the opposite approach. Those who are conscientious, and do want to please God, in response to His surpassing mercy, are then tempted — quite contrary to the Beatitudes, and to the fruits of the Spirit — to spin for themselves vast webs of spiritualizing fantasies and self-chosen observances, which may dazzle and impress but are otherwise of no earthly or heavenly use. Thus arise ever new versions of monasticism — like the New Pentecostalism! Let Luther bring us down to earth and point us to the Ten Commandments:

> It seems to me that all hands would be fully occupied just keeping these, gentleness, patience, love towards enemies, chastity, helpful acts, etc., and whatever is connected with such things. But such works don't rate or seem like much in the world's eyes. For they are not rare and puffed up, bound to their own special time, place, manner, and gesture, but are ordinary daily housework, such as one neighbor can practice towards another; therefore they command no great reward. But those other works arrest eyes and ears, besides they help themselves with much ostentation, cost, and magnificent structure, and ornament them, so that everything must gleam and shine; there they use incense, sing and ring, light candles and lights, so that before these works no others can be seen or heard. For when a priest stands there in a golden chasuble, or a layman spends all day in church on his knees, that is called a precious work, which no one can praise enough. But when a poor maid takes care of a young child and faithfully does as she is told, that must count for nothing . . . But look, is it not an accursed presumption of the desperate saints, who dare to find a higher and better life and conditions than the Ten Commandments teach...? (*Large Catechism*, Commandments, 313-315).

104. We need again and again to come face to face with the real de-

mands of God, that we may be driven by the divine earthquake from the comfortable shelters of our religious routines and our conventional respectabilities. Dwarfed and crushed by the mountain of His holiness — at once so necessary and commanded, and yet so infinitely unattainable — we stand before Him alone, defenseless, and inexcusable. We plead in Peter's words: "Depart from me, for I am a sinful man, O Lord" — only to find, with Luther, that the righteousness of God is first and foremost His free and saving gift in Jesus! And so it is that we learn to crave, with the insistence of newborn babies, the pure Word-milk of God, that by it we may thrive (I Pet. 2:2)!

2. Gift and Treasure

105. The world sees clergymen mainly in two stereotypes: either as sulphur-and-brimstone doomsayers straight from Mt. Sinai, or else as "bleeding heart" social gospel "do-gooders" with a ridiculous penchant for the latest secular fadlet! In conscious opposition to these decay-products of Puritanism, the Evangelical Lutheran pastor must see himself, and be seen, as the "steward of the mysteries of God" (1 Cor. 4:1, cf. *Apology*, XXIV, 80), the servant of Him Who came to be Savior to sinners. Physician to the sick, Help and Hope to the poor and lost. This means that as proclaimer of "Law and Gospel" the Lutheran pastor can never forget that the two terms of this phrase do not possess equal weight, stature, and dignity. One is subservient to the other, even as the permanent, New Covenant ministry of righteousness has far greater splendor than the temporary ministry of condemnation, engraved on stone (II Cor. 3:2-18)! The *Apology*, following Luther, expresses this by calling the Law, God's alien or "strange" work, while the Gospel is His very own or "proper" work (XII, 51-53). The terrors of the Law are there not for their own sake, but to plough and prepare the ground, to make it receptive to the seed of the Gospel, which alone is the bearer of life and salvation. This divinely ordained relationship must shape, direct, and sustain the entire public ministry of the Word and Sacraments. It must certainly determine the whole nature and intention of evangelical preaching.

106. Nothing is easier and more tempting than to preach moralizing sermons. Especially when the level of sanctification seems to us to be lagging far behind what we think it ought to be, the natural inclination is to resort to an endless nagging and wheedling with the Law — as if that could produce the fruits of the Spirit! The only solution is to preach Jesus into the hearts of people. Then they will love Him and willingly serve Him.

107. Only gradually, after years of preaching in the parish ministry, did it dawn on me how many people there are in our churches, precisely among the serious, conscientious members, who torment themselves with past guilt, and never quite dare to see themselves as fully accepted, absolved, and loved by God. Many such people never obtain the necessary relief from much of the preaching that goes on, which on the contrary, serves only to compound their sorrow and despair. We pastors must realize, with Luther, that devout consciences, under accusation by the Law,

do not readily believe themselves forgiven (*Apology*, IV, 250-164). They require the certain, firm, immovable promises and assurances of God Himself. And these need to be offered and proclaimed not hesitantly, or in small, grudging doses, but lavishly, continually, and in many different ways. Out of such preaching there flows into anxious souls a great and joyful confidence in Christ the Redeemer. Then the fearful devastations of unrelieved guilt are exorcised, and the miracle of forgiveness unleashes and boundless and upbuilding energies of true love and gratitude (St. Luke 7:36-50).

108. Rousas Rushdoony maintains that the average Reformed Sunday School is "subversive of all Christianity," because it "inculcates either outright Pelagianism and works salvation, as in liberal circles, or a Judaizing faith in conservative circles. Its effects are almost invariably moralistic, with atonement and cross simply "added on to goodness and works as the means of salvation." Do Lutheran Sunday Schools avoid these pitfalls? Unless the Sunday school teachers are properly trained and supervised by their pastors, they will lapse only too easily into the moralizing pattern ("The point of the story, dear children, is that Jesus loved and helped people, and so we should love and help people too"). Teachers need to be trained to see and appreciate the evangelical thrust and intent of the various Gospel pericopes. They also need to develop a keen sense of the intimate links between the New Testament text then and there in the past and its present realization here and now in the concrete means of grace of our church-life. The Reformed approach to New Testament events is: "This happened then and there, and now we remember it and think about it." The Lutheran, sacramental understanding of the text differs from this as totally as realism differs from symbolism: "This happened then and there, and we today do not merely remember it, but actually participate in it." Thus Baptism actually incorporates us into Christ's death and resurrection (Rom. 6:3 ff.; Col. 2:12). Through the absolution and Gospel-preaching of his appointed servant, the risen Savior Himself Who showed Himself to Thomas, again effectively repeats His greeting: "Peace be with you!" He is not far away "in heaven," but in and with His believers, assembled in His Name. The same holy body which Simeon held in his arms, is now distributed to us, so that we too "have seen (His) Salvation." As He touched, blessed, and healed the paralytic, the dropsical man, the deaf-mute, the woman with the issue of blood, the lepers, and even Lazarus and others who had died, so we today hear His self-same life-giving Shepherd's Voice in His Gospel, and receive the cleansing touch of His Real Presence, whereby we too are released from the leprosy, paralysis, misery, and death of our sins. All this presupposes of course the full sacramental realism of the New Testament, which we considered in the previous lecture.

109. In this way Justification, that is, God's acceptance of the sinner in Jesus, remains not simply one point among others, but the continuous and central thrust of our whole church-life, the focus of our appropriation and celebration of the mercies of God in Baptism, preaching, and Eucharist. Very helpful in this connection is the old Lutheran custom of

preaching on the Gospel for the Day at the main service, in this way the concrete Person of the Savior and His actual words and actions are immediately at the center of attention. Everything else must take its cue from there. Here the Vine supplies, cherishes, and renews His branches.

110. Not surprisingly, it is precisely concentrated pre-occupation with Gospel-riches, which provides the greatest impetus for sanctification. Why? Simply because, as the Lord explains, "he to whom little is forgiven, the same loveth little" (St. Luke 7:47). Generosity begets generosity, whilst scarcity compels even the noblest to economize. The first European refugees to leave a devastated Europe, after World War II, for the fabulous shores of America, were not accustomed to unrestricted supplies of sugar. And so they emptied the sugar-bowls of the ships' dining-room tables, and stuffed as much as they could into their pockets. They stopped this only when they were reassured that the supplies were plentiful, and saw the crew dumping sugar on the floor for sweeping up. So too we Christian absurdly claw and scratch about, anxiously stuffing our pockets with pebbles — when the whole universe is ours! Are we not heirs of God and joint-heirs with Christ? We will believe this and act accordingly only if these treasures are constantly preached and sealed into our hearts and minds. Small, unworthy notions of the goodness of God will in turn make us mean and grudging towards our fellow men. The more we grow in genuine appreciation of God's mercy, the more we ourselves are enabled to be merciful. Law-tormented Pharisees, on the other hand, cannot but torment others with the Law in turn.

111. What we are dealing with here is not mere religious psychology; it is deeply theological. The theology of it was spelled out by our Lord in the parable of the Prodigal Son, or rather, of the Elder Brother. The younger son, deeply conscious of his unworthiness, yet overwhelmed by fatherly mercy and love, now thinks the most menial work a precious privilege. We can imagine him kissing the very soil in gratitude — as Cuban refugees have done upon their safe arrival in America. Yet the older brother revealed by his reactions that he did not consider working for his father a joy and a privilege. To him it was dutiful drudgery. Basically, he envied his brother for his irresponsible spending spree. He might have done it himself had he had the courage or foreseen a safe reinstatement. He bitterly resented his brother for having, as it seemed, got "the best of both Worlds."

112. Here we see the eternal contrast between the Law oriented religion of the Pharisee and the mercy-motivated piety of the converted sinner. The former can have no pity or compassion for sinners; he basically envies and resents them for being somehow, if only perversely, more "fortunate." The latter can approach his former companions in evil with genuine compassion. He cannot envy them, for he understands only too well the terrible shackles of sin. He is no longer fooled by the glittering illusions of false freedom and self-fulfillment. Both men may work actively for the conversion of sinners—but from totally different motives. The Pharisee seeks to stop the scandal of other people enjoying pleasures, which he must, with gnashing teeth, deny himself. Their condition subtly

59

threatens and entices him, for deep down he regards it as preferable to his own hollow round of duties. The justified tax-collector, on the other hand, has actually found something genuinely and incomparably better, and is doing his best to share his new-found treasure with others. Whose mission-work is likely to have the greater credibility? The religiously ornamented natural man, that is to say the Pharisee, can indeed be stung into a veritable frenzy of proselytizing activity (St. Matt. 23:15) — only to ensnare others into his deadly cage. But the Good News of full and free pardon in Jesus can rescue captives from Satan's deepest and darkest dungeons, and can so wonderfully supply them, that others are bound to ask them, longingly, for the reason for the hope that is in them (I Peter 3:15)!

113. What a great pity that the religion of the Word is so often perceived as a religion of words! Why is it that the standard Sunday school response to the question, "What can we do to please God?" is something like: "Tell others about Jesus" (or worse, "teach others")? As if the practice of Christianity were first and foremost a matter of words and of verbalizing! To be sure, telling is an important aspect of discipleship — but only in the context of being and doing. While right talking does matter, mere talking lacks all integrity. Certainly the royal priesthood's praising of God in I Pet. 2:9 means something much more than merely "telling," or informing others (cf. v. 12 and the whole chapter), if justification is more than words, if indeed it opens to us all the treasure-roves of our generous God, then, wherever this is truly believed, the response will be far more than verbal. We will seek to be merciful, as we have received mercy. Luther does not hesitate to say that "just as He is Christ for us, we should also be Christ for them." As the Gospel-treasure is real, not imaginary, so it transforms our reality, not just our world of ideas. Says Luther:

> You should give yourself to your neighbor with your whole life, just as Christ does in the words of the Sacrament with all that He is ....We should say to our neighbor: "Dear brother, I have received my Lord and He is mine. I now have more than enough of everything. Take what I have; it is all yours. I place it at your disposal..."
> If you find that the words and the sign of the Sacrament are softening your heart and moving you to be kind to your enemy, to receive your neighbor, and to help him bear his distress and sorrow, all is well. If this is not the result of your partaking of the Sacrament, you cannot be certain that you have profited from the Sacrament, even if you were to partake of it a hundred times a day with the greatest devotion ... is also very dangerous, because it is so completely self-centered and misleading.[8]

114. The Chief Article of our Christian faith, by which the church either stands or falls, does not require human ingenuity and techniques to give it effect. It wins its own victories, far above all that we are able to ask or think, if it is but confessed, applied, and grasped, without human adulteration, it will achieve its God-given purpose:

For by grace are ye saved through faith, and that not of yourselves; it is the gift of God; Not of works, less any man should boast. For we are his workmanship, created in Christ Jesus unto good works, which God hath before ordained that we should walk in them. (Eph. 2:8-10).

Footnotes

1. H. J. Blackham, ed., *Objections to Humanism* (London: Constable, 1965), pp. 106-107.

2. Ibid.

3. Francis Schaeffer, *The God Who Is There* (London: Rodder and Stoughton, 1969), p. 42.

4. Lefferts E. Loetscher, *The Broadening Church* (Philadelphia: University of Pennsylvania Press, 1954), p. 9.

5. Paul Barnett and Peter Jensen, *The Quest for Power* (Sydney: Anzea, 1973).

6. Rousas J. Rushdoony, *Intellectual Schizophrenia* (Philadelphia: Presbyterian and Reformed, 1961), p. 121.

7. Paul D. Pahl, tr., *Luther for the Busy Man* (Adelaide: Lutheran Publishing House, 1974), p. 271.

8. Ibid., pp. 92-94.

Christian News, July 10, 1978

1. What was the subject of furious controversy in the 16th century? ____
2. Warren Quanbeck claimed that today theologians in both traditions can ____ on theological formulations without ____ their theological heritage.
3. Both Barth and Kueng make many ____ statements.
4. Kueng said that Protestants speak of ___ righteous and Roman Catholics of ___ righteous.
5. What was the most important item before the Council of Trent? ____
6. Did Christ earn man a chance to earn salvation? ____
7. "Faith" envisioned by Trent is purely ____.
8. What did Trent condemn? ____
9. Trent's Canon 10 condemns ____.
10. Good works, love, or sanctification are in no sense the basis of ____ before God.
11. What is not the ground or cause of acceptance before God? ____
12. Both the Apology and Formula of Concord exclude sanctification from ____.
13. What has become an anachronism today? ___
14. Why has it become an anachronism ? ____
15. Neither Rome nor Lutheranism have remained untouched by ____.
16. Whose heirs infest all major Western church bodies? ____
17. What can justification mean without the Resurrection of Christ? ____
18. "This ____ dominates the LWF and WCC."
19. In the 16th century what was taken for granted? ____

20. What false impression prevails today in the Anglo-Saxon world? ____
21. The Lutheran Confessions understand justification as the ____.
22. Every article of faith requires no proof by means of ____.
23. What did Bultmann, who insisted on "justification through faith alone," regard as legends? ____
24. What did the 1963 Assembly of the LWF say about justification? ____
25. Luther never meant that justification was the center to the exclusion of ____.
26. What is the divinely given center? ____
27. Present Truth wished to maintain ____.
28. A problem of Wesley's theology was ____.
29. Pentecostalism was an offshoot of ____.
30. The basic orientation of Present Truth is ____.
31. At its deepest level Pentecostalism is ____.
32. What does "Lutheran" Charismatic Larry Christenson cite? ____
33. There is not the slightest hint in the New Testament that "tongues" are supposed to ____.
34. One of Luther's central concerns was to overcome ____.
35. John Calvin taught the unbiblical notion of ____.
36. What is the absolute indispensable basis of certainty? ____
37. Calvinism cannot theoretically provide any firm defense against ____.
38. What is the dilemma in Francis Schaeffer's True Spirituality? ____
39. While many of our people are Lutheran in theory they are ____ in practice?
40. How can it be explained that the Living Bible has become immensely popular even among Lutherans? ____
41. What is the Pearl of great price? ____
42. Bonheffer was correct when he recognized that "salvation by grace" is ____.
43. It is futile and absurd to be forever ____.
44. What high and awesome art can we in this life be but humble ____.
45. One of the prime deficiencies of our age is ____.
46. One of the chief factors for the virtual evaporation of sin from the public mind is ____.
47. What is daily becoming more explicit? ____
48. If there is no God then ____.
49. What did Francis Schaefffer show in The God Who Is There? ____
50. What is the basic thrust of much contemporary literature and drama? ____
51. Popular sloganeering makes the word "Evangelical" mean ____.
52. What spawns such unspeakable offenses as "Lutheran" abortionists? ____
53. The denial of moral distinctions has become ____.
54. One of the prime seductions of "cheap grace" is ____.
55. Sin is sin only where ____.
56. What do people need from the Word of God? ____
57. The historic Liturgy is being pushed out for ____.
58. Did Luther's doctrine encourage moral laxity? ____

59. The righteousness of God is first and foremost ____.
60. The Evangelical Lutheran pastor must see himself as ____.
61. Devout consciences, under the accusation of the Law, do not readily see themselves as ____.
62. Rousas Rushdoony maintains that the average Reformed Sunday School is ____.
63. Sunday School teachers need to be trained to ____.
64. Baptism actually incorporates us into ____.
65. What provides the greatest impetus for sanctification? ____
66. The more we grow in general appreciation of God's mercy, the more we ____.
67. The religion of Word is often perceived as____.
68. The Chief Article of our Christian faith does not require ____.

JUSTIFICATION: LET'S BE SPECIFIC

The chief defect of the US Lutheran/Roman Catholic statement on Justification is that it fails to settle the central issue; is justification forgiveness or also internal improvement? Apart from that, the chief "sticking point" no doubt is the place of justification as a litmus test for all faith and practice in the church. "The Lutheran movement," the document rightly reports, "founded at a time when superstition and corruption were rampant, was legitimately concerned to find a critical principle by which to test what is authentically Christian" (#117). There is no better example of how this actually works, than Luther's own Smalcald Articles of 1537.

The Roman Catholic side, on the other hand, "are wary of using any one doctrine as the absolute principle by which to purify from the outside, so to speak, the [Roman] Catholic heritage" (#118).

Now it is true, of course, that some of the crasser features of medieval "superstition and corruption" have been cleaned up. Indeed, liturgical reform within Roman Catholicism has dampened enthusiasm even for such things as rosaries. Oddly enough the New World lags behind Europe in this respect. That at least seems to be the point of a reference by Nikolaus Lobkowicz, former president of the University of Munich, to American tourists carrying rosaries, "which in Germany, for example, have become almost extinct, except in small villages" (*News-Weekly* [Australia], 18 April 1984).

The issue is not academic. To be more than words on "patient paper," any real agreement on justification would have to include the provision that contrary beliefs and practices are to be corrected. It would have to come clean for instance on whether the following Sample of the Sacred Heart cult is evangelical or superstitious. A Sacred Heart Monastery in Wisconsin quotes, "with ecclesiastical approbation," as authentic words of the Savior:

> I promise thee in the excessive mercy of My Heart that My all-powerful love will grant to all those who communicate on the First Friday in nine consecutive months the grace of final penitence; they shall not die in My disgrace nor without receiving their Sacraments.

Further it is claimed: "All Auxiliary members share in the graces earned through the prayers and good works of the Priests and Brothers of the Sacred Heart."

"Rosaries for Peace"

The latest issue of Divine Love, published by the Apostolate Of Christian Action in Fresno, California, is a "'Rosaries For Peace' Issue." All articles appearing in Divine Love are first cleared through a diocesan censor "to make sure they contain nothing contrary to faith or morals."

The editor of this Roman Catholic publication claims that at various times in history "Christianity was spared through the power of prayer, particularly the Rosary." He writes: "In addition to the ominous Soviet military build-up, to us, there is another major indication of how critical the world situation really is, and the urgent need for many prayers and sacrifices for peace at this time. We refer to the requests of Pope John Paul II for public 'Rosaries For Peace' rallies, to be held throughout the United States, from July 15th until the end of October, 1984, as reported in our last issue of DIVINE LOVE."

According to the article titled "Rosaries For Peace," "God wills that peace comes through prayer, sacrifice, and a return to His Commandments. But He cannot and will not interfere with our free will. In other words, on the one hand, the more sin and evil that results from our own misuse of free will, the greater success Satan has. On the other hand, the more Masses, Holy Communions, Rosaries, sacrifices, and reparations for sin, that we offer up to *God,* the more effectively He can 'check-mate' Satan and his plans to destroy the world, the Church, and souls."

"Almighty God sent His Mother and ours to Fatima, Portugal, in 1917, to give to the world HIS 'peace plan from Heaven.' At Fatima, Our Lady told the three little shepherd children (and us), that for peace, 'People MUST say the Rosary; let them continue saying it every day.' In other words, the daily Rosary is one of God's primary conditions for true world peace.

"If enough people grant God's request for the daily Rosary, there will eventually be true peace. If not, one shudders to think of what the future holds for America and the world."

A two-page article in Divine Love titled "A Nationwide Crusade of 'Rosaries For Peace'" says: "When we announced in our last issue, (No. 93), that a nation-wide 'Rosaries For Peace' crusade would be launched throughout the United States, from July 15-October 31,1984, we had no idea what to expect. The project was decided upon in May, 1984, on very short notice. It came after Bishop Constantino Luna, O.F.M., International President of the Blue Army of Our Lady of Fatima, returned to the U.S., after a private audience with the Holy Father in March.

"During that audience, Pope John Paull II made known his wish for a Rosary crusade, particularly in the United States."

"The first official program took place on Sunday, July 15. It was held at the new Immaculate Heart of Mary Shrine, at Our Lady of Peace Church in Santa Clara, California. On a warm, sunny afternoon, more than 1,000 people from throughout California gathered around Our Lady's towering statue, to pray the Rosary for peace; to participate in the Holy Sacrifice of the Mass, and receive Jesus in Holy Communion; and to concentrate themselves to the Immaculate Heart of Mary, especially through wearing or enrolling in the Brown Scapular. It was a simple, beautiful, and inspiring ceremony.

"Since then, many additional 'Rosaries For Peace' programs have been organized and scheduled to the end of October — more than 200 in all."

Our Lady of Fatima

Divine Love says that "It seems almost as if Our Lady herself, has taken charge of this 'Rosaries For Peace' crusade." "As Nineveh responded to Jonah, so we must respond to Our Lady of Fatima. History demonstrates that entire civilizations have been saved through the power of the Rosary — our perfect weapon. Salvation from nuclear destruction does not lie in building more nuclear weapons, but in the miraculous power of prayer."

"Most of the 'Rosaries For Peace' programs include the praying of the Rosary; the Holy Sacrifice of the Mass; enrollment in the Brown Scapular; and consecration to the Immaculate Heart of Mary."

We are photographing here an article by Pope John Paul I on the rosary and "Fatima And Rosary Projects" from the Roman Catholic Divine Love magazine.

Disavow Innovations

If the Roman Catholic Church now really accepts the scriptural doctrine of justification by faith alone it would disavow such innovations as the rosary, purgatory, prayers to saints and Mary, etc.

Luther noted that it was nonsense to claim that the Reformation introduced entirely new points of view. "This message is not a novel invention of ours but the very ancient, approved teaching of the apostles brought to light again. Neither have we invented a new Baptism, Sacrament of the Altar, Lord's Prayer, and Creed; nor do we desire to know or to have anything new in Christendom. We only contend for, and hold to, the ancient; that which Christ and the apostles have left behind them and have given us to do."

Luther wrote: "Tell me, is not the private Mass a shameful innovation? Why, then, was its introduction allowed, and why do you still defend it? Indeed, if no innovation had been allowed, what and how much would we now find among you that is found in the ancient canons and in the fathers? Why, I could enclose it in a nutshell, while your innovations have filled the world, I will even say more. What was your church life before our Gospel came but daily innovations? One after another they broke in, piles of them, like a cloudburst. One set up St. Anne; another St. Christopher; another, St. George; another, St. Barbara; another, St. Bastian; another, St. Catherine; another, the Fourteen Protectors. And who can tell the tale of this new saint worship alone? Are these not innovations? Where were the bishops then, and the people who cry out, whose duty it was not to allow such things? But more. One set up the rosary; another, the crown of Mary; one, the Psalter of Mary; another the ten paternoster stones on the church doors; another the prayers to St. Bridget; one, this prayer; another, that prayer, all without number of measure, and all books full of this stuff. Where was a bishop or a doctor who would look at least a little cross-eyed at such innovation?" (*What Luther Says*, Concordia, 1959, pp. 1180-1).

Luther, of course, did not go along with the radicals who wanted to expel everything from the church for which chapter and verse from Scripture could not be quoted. He opposed those who broke statues and stained glass windows. He was glad to keep anything that did not offend against the word of God. He told some Anabaptist preachers: "Now we do confess that much Christian good, nay, all Christian good, is to be found in the papacy and from there it has descended to us. For we confess that in the papacy the true Holy Scripture, the true Baptism, the true Sacrament of the Altar, the true keys and forgiveness of sins, the true office of the ministry, the true Catechism, as the Ten Commandments, the articles of the Creed, and the Lord's Prayer, exist."

"We do not act as fanatically as the sectarian spirits; we do not reject everything that is under the dominion of the pope. For in that event we should also reject the Christian Church, the temple of God, with everything it has received from Christ. But what we do attack and condemn is the fact that the Pope will not rest content with the blessings of the Christian Church, which he has inherited from the apostles. On the contrary, he adds and imposes his diabolic innovations and does not use the apostolic blessings for the improvement of God's temple but for its destruction; he causes his own law and ordinance to be esteemed more highly than the ordinance of Christ. Amid this destruction Christ nonetheless preserves His church, just as He protected Lot at Sodom, as St. Peter declares concerning this matter (2 Peter 2:6-7). In consequence, both remain a fact: the Antichrist sits in the temple of God through the working of Satan (2 Thess. 2:4-9), and yet the temple of God continues to be the temple of God through the preservation wrought by Christ. . ." (*What Luther Says,* p. 1182).

The rosary and prayers to Mary are among the papal innovations which Rome will have to repudiate before it can truly be said that Rome accepts the scriptural doctrine of justification by faith alone in the merits of Jesus Christ. We plead with our Roman Catholic friends, particularly those who are so opposed to theological modernism, to disavow all of the modernistic innovations, especially the doctrine of justification by faith and works, which have infiltrated their church. Until Rome returns to the doctrines of Holy Scripture and the faith of the ancient Christian Church it remains a modernistic sect.

Christian News, October 22, 1984

1. What is the chief defect of the U.S. Lutheran/Roman Catholic statement on Justification? ____
2. What has become almost extinct in Germany? ____
3. According to Rome, what happened at Fatima? ____
4. If the Roman Catholic Church now accepts justification by faith alone, then ____.
5. Luther wrote that "We only contend for ___."
6. Luther did not go along with those who ____.
7. He opposed those who ____.
8. Luther said that the Pope adds ____.
9. What did Luther say about the Anti-Christ? ____

67

NO "HOAX"
MAIER AND OBJECTIVE JUSTIFICATION

Allow me to address a few remarks to the matters raised by my esteemed brother-in-office, Pastor Vernon Harley, in his article, "Problems with 'Objective' Justification" (CN 8, June 1981).

When discussions become inflamed to the degree that the Objective Justification debate clearly has, one needs to pay heed not simply to what is said, but also to what is perceived as being said.

One fears that despite some safeguarding language, Pastor Harley's article may be perceived as defending Dr. Walter A. Maier by attacking objective justification, and not simply the terminology, but the doctrine itself. Two observations are in order:

1. The impression should not be given that "objective justification" is a technical subtlety originating in 19th century U.S. Lutheran squabbles among Norwegians, Swedes, and the Missouri and Ohio synods. Whatever the terminology, the doctrine itself is at the very heart of Lutheran theology, where grace alone is confessed against Romanism, universal grace against Calvinism, and the means of grace against both.

The whole Lutheran notion of "special faith" (Apol. XII, 45, 59), which is "conceived of the Gospel or absolution" (CA XII) presupposes a real, objective treasure of forgiveness (Apol. IV, 103-105) brought into existence for all men by the work of Christ, and really and truly offered, distributed, and communicated to them in the means of grace, to be appropriated and received by faith alone. And this grand conception was, in German, inevitably cast in the language which had become normative through the Luther Bible's rendering of Rom. 5:18 and 2 Cor. 5:19.

2. The crisp, precise sentences of Dr. Walter A. Maier's public statement of 31 January 1981 confess objective justification in the clearest possible terms:

"When the Lord Jesus was 'justified' (1 Timothy 3:16) in His resurrection and exaltation, God acquitted Him not of sins of His own, but of all the sins of mankind, which as the Lamb of God He had been bearing (John 1:29), and by the imputation of which He had been 'made... to be sin for us' (2 Cor. 5:21), indeed 'made a curse for us' (Gal. 3:13).

"In this sense the justification of Jesus was the justification of those whose sins He bore. The treasure of justification or forgiveness gained by Christ for all mankind is truly offered, given, and distributed in and through the Gospel and the sacraments of Christ.

"Faith alone can receive this treasure offered in the Gospel, and this faith itself is entirely a gracious gift and creation of God through the means of grace. Faith adds nothing to God's forgiveness in Christ offered in the Gospel, but only receives it. Thus, 'He that believeth on the Son hath everlasting life; and he that believeth not the Son, shall not see life; but the wrath of God abideth on Him' (John 3:36)."

(This parallels rather closely the pivotal 3rd thesis of the 1872 Synodical Conference essay on Justification: "In the pure doctrine of justification, as our Lutheran Church has presented it again from God's Word and placed it on the lampstand, it is above all a matter of three points: 1. Of the doctrine of the general, perfect redemption (Erloesung) of the world through Christ; 2. Of the doctrine of the power and efficacy of the means of grace, and 3. Of the doctrine of faith.").

Dr. Maier quotes from that 1872 essay:

"When speaking with regard to the acquisition of salvation (by Christ), God has wrath for no man any longer; but when speaking with regard to the appropriation. He is wrathful with everyone who is not in Christ (*Proceedings*, p. 32).

"Before faith the sinner is righteous before God only according to the acquisition and the divine intention, but he is actually (**actu**) righteous, righteous for his own person, righteous indeed, first when he believes (*Proceedings*, p. 68)."

These necessary distinctions function — in the original 1872 essay as well as in Dr. Maier's statement — not as denials of objective justification, but as explanations of how this matter has always been understood in our church.

How in these circumstances these references can be construed as a "hoax" is as incomprehensible to me as it is to Pastor Harley. The trouble is that this unfounded charge gains plausibility if in rebutting it we in any way suggest that objective justification is something less than Biblical, Reformation truth.

Yours faithfully,
K.E. Marquart, Associate Professor
Concordia Theological Seminary
Fort Wayne, Indiana
Christian News, July 6, 1981

1. Is "Objective justification" a technical subtlety originating in 19th century U.S. Lutheran squabbles? ____
2. Walter A. Maier said in 1981 ____ adds nothing to God's forgiveness in Christ but only ____.
3. Man is righteous before God when he first ____.
4. Is objective justification something less than Biblical, Reformation truth? ____.

"OBJECTIVE JUSTIFICATION"

Editor's Note: When Kurt Marquart died in 2006, William Bischoff, pastor of Trinity Lutheran Church, Bridgeton, Missouri wrote:

"Kurt Marquart will long be remembered as a great scholar, theologian, and seminary professor. Many of the active clergy in the Lutheran Church- Missouri Synod once sat at his feet as they studied for the ministry. They were all impressed by his rare ability to take the most difficult theological subject and encapsulate ponderous terminology into a finished product that was clear and simple, as well as concise.

"Kurt Marquart knew that he had been saved to serve with both love and humility. As a seminary professor in the public arena and in his private relationships that inner depth of love and humility were manifest. Our congregation in Missouri once offered him $1000 to prepare a lengthy paper clarifying the doctrine of objective justification. Many hours of labor were invested in this project. When it was finished he requested our congregation send the money to aid a third world student at the seminary. His tireless efforts in the mission fields of Haiti and Russia are well known. (Marquart's Legacy, p. 25)

* * *

Having been asked by Trinity Church, Bridgeton, Missouri, for a theological analysis of certain papers by Mr. Larry Darby on the subject of "objective justification," I herewith submit my findings, first of all with profound regrets for the long delay, and secondly with the humble prayer that anything now said may still be of help to Christian consciences struggling with this issue.

Given the high level of conflict that has ensued in this matter, I have attempted scrupulously to restrict my remarks to matters of fact and theology, and to avoid inflammatory rhetoric or judgments about motives. I am conscious of no ill will or prejudice against anyone involved in this dispute.

By way of a basic frame of reference I shall first sketch out the standard Lutheran perspective on justification, as found above all in the Book of Concord itself, together with its biblical basis, and then evaluate Mr. Darby's arguments in that context, spelling out specific agreements and disagreements with his theses.[1]

1. A Digression on Terminology

I agree with Henry Hamann that the terminology "objective/subjective justification" is less than ideal since "subjective justification . . . is every whit as objective as objective justification."[2]

On the other hand, when Calvinists use the same terminology, it expresses *their* meaning very well: "Passive or subjective justification takes place in the heart or conscience of the sinner."[3] The Reformed reject *universal grace,* hence cannot mean *general justification* by "objective justification;" and "subjective justification" means for them something *experiential* precisely what it does not mean for Lutherans. Biblically, justification is God's act, which faith receives or believes, but does not feel or "experience."

To avoid these problems, it would be best to retain the more traditional usage, which spoke of the "general justification" of the world in Christ and of the "personal justification" of individual sinners through faith alone. This corresponds exactly to the biblical distinction between God's own completed reconciliation of the world to Himself in Christ (II Cor. 5: 19) and our reconciliation to him by faith (v. 20).

If the sense is clear, one should not quarrel about words. The "visible/invisible" terminology in respect of the church is a case in point. Our Confessions do not use that language, but speak of the church in the "proper sense" and in the "wide sense." Moreover, Calvinists mean something quite different and unbiblical when *they* speak of "visible" and "invisible" churches. Yet standard Lutheran theology since Gerhard has spoken of the church being "visible" and "invisible," and meant the right, orthodox content by this terminology. Similarly one must assume—other things being equal-that when orthodox Lutheran theologians speak of "objective" and "subjective" justification, they mean to express biblical, confessional truth, and not Calvinist or other deviations.

2. The Standard Lutheran Pattern in Presenting Justification

The best starting point is *Formula of Concord (Solid Declaration)* III:25:

The only essential and necessary elements of justification are the grace of God, the merit of Christ, and faith which accepts these in the promise of the Gospel (Tappert, p. 543 , compare *Apology* IV:53, p. 114).

We may put these essential ingredients of justification into a list, as follows:

1. The grace of God
2. The merit of Christ
3. The promise of the Gospel
4. Faith

The first three items constitute what was later called "objective justification." The addition of faith completes the list, which thus defines justification in the full, normal biblical and ecclesiastical sense and usage. This *ordinary* sense of the word is labeled "subjective" (individual, personal) only in contexts requiring a distinction from the *special* usage of "objective" (general, universal) justification.

But why did such a distinction arise at all?

By stripping away the surrounding words, we obtain the following sequence in *Augsburg Confession* IV (German): "we receive forgiveness of sin ... when we believe ... that for [Christ's] sake our sin is forgiven" (Tappert, p. 30).

Apology IV explains, repeatedly, that "when a man believes that his sins are forgiven because of Christ and that God is reconciled and favorably disposed to him because of Christ, this personal faith *[fides specialis]* obtains the forgiveness of sins and justifies us" (45, compare 48, 56, 62, 82, 103, 178, 195, 279, 299 [garbled in Tappert, p. 153], 345, 379, 381, 382, 386, and XII, 45, 59, 60, 61 , 62, 63-65, 74, 76, 88, and XIII, 21).

The pattern is clear and consistent throughout: the Gospel or absolution offers not a conditional, future prospect, but a perfected, past and present reality. God already is gracious, merciful, propitious, reconciled in Christ, and freely offers this ready forgiveness or grace in the Gospel. To believe this Gospel or absolution is to believe *oneself* forgiven, justified, accepted. Forgiveness exists "objectively" already before faith. Faith does not create forgiveness but only receives, accepts, appropriates it. Absolution is prior to, and creates faith, not vice versa *(Augsburg Confession* XII, 5; *Apology* XII, 42). The Gospel "offers forgiveness and justification, which are received by faith" *(Apology* IV, 62). And: "forgiveness of sins is the same as justification" (IV, 76).

At just this point the Roman adversaries, particularly Cardinal Bellarmine, thought they had found a fatal flaw and self-contradiction in the Lutheran system: You say that you are justified by faith, they argued, yet you also say that faith must believe that one has been forgiven already; so when is one forgiven or justified then, before faith, or in faith? Surely both can't be true.

This objection compelled the Lutherans to explain in what sense forgiveness exists already *prior* to faith, as its object, and to distinguish that from the actual reception, possession, and enjoyment of the pre-existing treasure, which happens only *in* faith. Calov's classic commentary on the Augsburg Confession (1665) put it like this:

[Justification] is the *object* of faith in that it is offered by God in the Gospel; it is the *effect* [of faith] to put it thus, in so far as grace having been apprehended by faith, the forgiveness of sins happens to us by that very act.

John Benedict Carpzov's *Introduction to the Symbolical Books of the Lutheran Churches* spells this out in greater detail:

The forgiveness of sins is considered in a *twofold manner. First,* as it has been *acquired* by Christ and is *offered* as a benefit *promised* and intended by God for sinners, to be sought and had in the Word and Sacraments. *Afterwards* [forgiveness is considered] as it has already been *accepted* by faith, has been applied, and is possessed. . . In the *first* manner the forgiveness of sins is the *object* of faith *insofar as it justifies . . .*[4]

It is this necessary and fundamental distinction, without which it is not possible to explain *"faith alone"* and the proper *function* of faith in justification, which was always the point of all standard Lutheran talk about "objective" or general and "subjective" or personal justification. The terms may be recent, but they express and safeguard nothing other than "the catechismal doctrine plain":

The work is finished and completed, Christ has acquired and won the treasure for us by His sufferings, death, and resurrection, etc. But if the work remained hidden and no one knew of it, it would have been all in vain, all lost. In order that this treasure might not be buried but put to use and enjoyed, God has caused the Word to be published and proclaimed, in which he has given the Holy Spirit to offer and apply to us this treasure of salvation *(Large Catechism,* Creed, 38).

Although the work was accomplished and forgiveness of sins was acquired on the cross, yet it cannot come to us in any other way than through the Word. Now, the whole Gospel and the article of the Creed, "I believe one holy Christian church, the forgiveness of sins," etc., are by the Word placed into this Sacrament and set before us... The treasure is opened and placed at everyone's door, yes, upon everyone's table, but what goes with it, is that you also attend to it and with certainty assent to it, as the words give [it] to you (Sacrament of the Altar, 31, 32, 35, slightly correcting Tappert's text, p. 450).

3. The Biblical Basis of "Objective/Subjective Justification"

Rather than rehash "in-house" exegesis, let us look at the relevant biblical material as displayed by Hans Kueng, a world-class, liberal Roman Catholic New Testament scholar, who stands entirely outside any and all Lutheran debates. The following extended quotations are from chapter 29 of Kueng's book *Justification,*[5] *which* seeks to reconcile the Council of Trent with Karl Barth! Not the slightest, "Missourian" connection here! Although Barth had an enormous, yet not uncritical respect for Luther, the Council of Trent certainly did not. It is difficult to imagine a doctrinal stance more hostile to "objective justification" than that of the Council of Trent. Against this background Kueng's reading of the biblical text, and his citation of other Roman Catholic exegetes in support, are all the more impressive (all emphases in original):

29. JUSTIFICATION IN CHRIST'S DEATH AND RESURRECTION
. . . But when is the sinner declared just? When does God's gracious saving judgment of the sinner occur? . . . But for Sacred Scripture the real judgment of God is inexorably bound up with the crucifixion and resurrection of Jesus Christ. In *the death and resurrection of Jesus Christ* the sinner is declared just: "But now the righteousness of God has been manifested ... the righteousness of God through faith in Jesus Christ for all who believe. For there is no distinction; since all have sinned and fall short of the glory of God, they are *justified* by his grace as a gift, through the *redemption* which is in Christ Jesus, whom God

73

put forward as an expiation by his blood, to be received by faith. This was to show God's righteousness, because in his divine forbearance he had passed over former sins; it was to prove at the present time that he himself is righteous and that he justifies him who has faith in Jesus" (Rom. 3.21-26). We are *"justified* by his *blood"* (Rom. 5.9); Christ "was put to death for our trespasses and *raised* for our *justification"* (Rom. 4.25) . . . (p. 222).

In reading texts which speak of justification in connection with the death and resurrection of Jesus Christ, it is striking to note that all of them referred emphatically to *faith* as well (for example, Rom. 4.5, 20'25). Only he who believes is justified. The task consequently is to relate the "objective" act of justification which happened on the cross with its "subjective" realization. On the one hand, the justification accomplished on the cross must not be separated from the process which reaches down to the individual man: this would in one way or another lead to apokatastasis [(universal) restoration, universalism, K.M.]. On the other hand, personal justification must not be separated from the general act of justification on the cross; this would in one way or another lead to predestinationism. Rather both must be seen as the two sides of a single truth: *All* men are justified in Jesus Christ and only *the faithful* are justified in Jesus Christ. The generic act of justification on the cross is the "permanently actual presence of salvation, accessible for personal appropriation" (Schrenk, S.V. in *TWNT [Theologisches Woerterbuch zum Neuen Testament]*, II, 220f.). The divine character of the declaration of divine justice and grace which took place on the cross once and for all and for all men, makes possible a relation between "objective" and "subjective" justification.

It is the task of this chapter to stress the "objective" aspect of justification ...

This, therefore, is the event: In the death and resurrection of Jesus Christ, God's gracious saving judgment on sinful mankind is promulgated. Here God pronounces the gracious and life-giving judgment which causes the one just man to be sin and in exchange makes all sinners free in Him: "He [God] made him to be sin who knew no sin, so that in him we might become the righteousness of God" (2 Cor. 5.21; cf. Gal. 3.13; Rom. 8.3). And in this ("objective") sense we can say that through Jesus Christ all men are justified, because "one has died for all" (2 Cor. 5.14; cf. 1 Tim. 2.6). "Then as one man's trespass led to condemnation for all men, so one man's act of righteousness leads to acquittal and life for all men. For as by one man's disobedience many were made sinners, so by one man's obedience many will be made righteous" (Rom. 5.18-19; cf. 5.12-17; 8.32; 11.32). ... (223-224).

In the Pauline perspective especially, justification never stands in isolation as a purely personal event; it has its place in the total framework of salvation history, of the redemption of all mankind. Those justified on the cross and in the resurrection are "the many," the "all."

The object of justification, as the prophets proclaimed, is Israel, the people of God, and in the new Israel, all people on earth. In Jesus Christ all men were justified and thereby called to the Church and even germinally integrated into it. . . Through faith, the individual shares the general justification, and so justification, as it occurs in the death and resurrection of Jesus Christ, is essentially *ecclesiological* in character... (224-225).

"The objective fact of justification is accomplished in the redemptive death of Christ, in connection, of course, with the resurrection. And so Rom. 5.9 can insist that we are justified in His blood, and by way of complement, in Rom. 4.25, that Christ was raised up for our justification" (Meinertz, *Theologie des NT,* II, 116). Catholic theologians do not normally speak of justification in connection with the death and resurrection of Christ. They prefer to the term "justification" (which is ordinarily understood as "subjective") the terms "redemption," "atonement," and so forth. But we saw that the term "justification" is used here in perfect agreement with scripture, revealing a deep and ultimately indispensable meaning .. . (226).

. .. what Barth and with him many Protestants call "justification" largely coincides with what we Catholics call "redemption" and . . . many expressions that sound heretical ought to be understood as completely orthodox (e.g., *"all* men are justified in Christ," although it agrees with Scripture may seem to Catholic ears to imply apokatastasis which Barth, however, categorically rejects. In ordinary Catholic usage — and in agreement with scripture — this would mean nothing other than the totally orthodox statement that *"All* men are *'redeemed'* in or by Jesus Christ.")... Everything does indeed depend on the proper definition of the relationship between "objective" and "subjective" justification ... (227-228).

Put without polemics then, the justification of the sinner means the declaration of justice by God who at the cross and in the resurrection of Jesus Christ declares all sinners free and just, and thereby makes them just, though this act can, for the Church, have its consequences in the individual only if the individual submits in faith to God's verdict... Only thus is adequate weight given to the *theocentricity* of justification. It is not primarily a matter of a process of salvation taking place within man. . . Rather the primary issue is the wrath and grace of *God, His* divine act of gracious and judicial decision, of justification considered as active; it is not primarily "peace to men on earth," but "glory to God in the highest." It is not primarily the justification of man, whereby man receives justice, but the *self-justification of God,* whereby God, willing from eternity salvation and creation, is proven just.

"Therefore say to the house of Israel, Thus says the Lord God: It is *not* for your sake, O house of Israel, that I am about to act, but for the sake of my holy name, which you have profaned among the nations to which you came. And I will vindicate the holiness of my great name, which has been profaned ... among them; and the nations will know that *I* am the LORD, says the Lord God, when through you I vindicate my holiness before their eyes" (Ezek. 36.22-23; cf. 36.31-32; Rom. 3.26).

Thus the accent is not on the "subjective" but on the "objective" aspect of justification. It is true that everything depends on this having its effect within individual men, on its realization in the individual, on human participation in it. It is true, too, that only he who believes is actually (subjectively) justified. Yet the decisive element in the sinner's justification is found not in the individual but in the death and resurrection of Christ. It was there that our situation was actually changed; there the essential thing happened. What afterwards happened in the individual man would be impossible to conceive of in isolation. It is not man in his faith who originally changes the situation, who does the essential thing. It is not a matter of completion of the central salvation event in Jesus Christ, but rather an active acknowledgment, and this solely by the power stemming from the central event ... In the death and resurrection of Christ, justification is established with final validity. It has happened once and for all and irrevocably (230-231).

When due allowance has been made in some details for Kueng's captivity to the Council of Trent, one can hardly improve on his deployment of the biblical material to our topic.

Kueng's reference to God's self-vindication suggests especially I Tim. 3: 15: "He was manifest in the flesh, justified in the Spirit..." What can it mean that Our Lord was "justified"? Since He had no sins of His own, but had, as Lamb of God, died a criminal's death for the sins of the world, He, and therefore that world in Him, was "justified" or "vindicated" by His holy Resurrection. Compare the very similar contrasts in I Peter 3: 18: put to death/flesh-made alive/spirit.

While elsewhere the *Apology* "allegorizes" Col. 2: 14, so as to apply it to "subjective" justification (IV,350; XII, 48), in IV, 103 the text is clearly taken in its original sense, in which it refers to the world-embracing justification-event of the Cross: "when the Lord Jesus came He forgave all men the sin that none could escape and by shedding his blood canceled the bond that stood against us [Col. 2: 14]. This is what Paul says, 'Law came in, to increase the trespass; but where sin increased, grace abounded all the more' [Rom. 5:20] through Jesus. For after the whole world was subjected, He took away the sin of the whole world, as John testified when he said [John 1:29]. 'Behold the Lamb of God, Who takes away the sin of the world!'" This is quoted from St. Ambrose, with the comment that this one pronouncement [Tappert's "sentence" is inaccurate] by St. Ambrose does more for the right understanding of St. Paul than all the opinions of illustrious scholastics put together!

Both the "objective" and the "subjective" aspects of the biblical understanding of justification are well captured in this balanced definition of

76

the *Formula of Concord,* Art. III, 4:

> Against both parties it was unanimously preached by the other teachers of the Augsburg Confession that Christ is our Righteousness not only according to the divine nature, and not only according to the human nature, but according to both natures, Who as God and Man has redeemed, justified, and saved us from our sins by His perfect obedience: so that the righteousness of faith is forgiveness of sins, reconciliation with God, and that we are adopted as children of God for the sake of the sole obedience of Christ, which is imputed as righteousness to all who truly believe, only through faith, from pure grace, and they are absolved for the sake of the same from all their unrighteousness [my translation, as literal as I can make it].

True, without faith no one benefits one whit. But in the Bible, as Kueng reminded us, "the accent is not on the 'subjective' but on the 'objective' aspect of justification .... the decisive element in the sinner's justification is found not in the individual but in the death and resurrection of Christ.... there the essential thing happened." The *Smalcald Articles* faithfully reflect this:

> The first and chief article is this, that Jesus Christ, our God and Lord, "was put to death for our trespasses and raised again for our justification" (Rom. 4:25). He alone is "the Lamb of God, who takes away the sin of the world" (John 1:29). "God has laid upon him the iniquities of us all" (Isa. 53:6). Moreover, "all have sinned," and "they are justified by his grace as a gift, through the redemption which is in Christ Jesus, by his blood" (Rom. 3:23-25).
>
> Inasmuch as this must be believed and cannot be obtained or apprehended by any work, law, or merit, it is clear and certain that such faith alone justifies us, as St. Paul says in Romans 3, "For we hold that a man is justified by faith apart from works of law" (Rom. 3:28), and again, "that he [God] himself is righteous and that he justifies him who has faith in Jesus" (Rom. 3:26).
>
> Nothing in this article can be given up or compromised, even if heaven and earth and things temporal should be destroyed. For as St. Peter says, "There is no other name under heaven given among men by which we must be saved" (Acts 4: 12). "And with his stripes we are healed" (Isa. 53:5).
>
> On this article rests all that we teach and practice against the pope, the devil, and the world. Therefore we must be quite certain and have no doubts about it. Otherwise all is lost, and the pope, the devil, and all our adversaries will gain the victory (WI, Tappert, p. 292).

4. Defensible Theses of Mr. Larry Darby:

(a) That the "Kokomo" notions about Judas and other inmates of hell being declared "innocent" and granted "the sta-

77

tus of saints," are an absurd and reprehensible travesty of Lutheran doctrine.

It is mind-boggling that any Lutheran could ever have written such stuff, and Mr. Darby is completely right to denounce it as the mischievous nonsense which it is.

Here are the four "Kokomo" theses forced on some hapless Indiana Lutherans (Wisconsin Synod) in 1979, on pain of excommunication:

1. Objectively speaking, without any reference to an individual sinner's attitude toward Christ's sacrifice, purely on the basis of God's verdict, every sinner, whether he knows it or not, whether he believes it or not, has received the status of a saint.

2. After Christ's intervention and through Christ's intervention, God regards all sinners as guilt-free saints.

3. When God reconciled the world to Himself through Christ, He individually pronounced forgiveness on each individual sinner whether that sinner ever comes to faith or not.

4. At the time of the resurrection of Christ, God looked down in hell and declared Judas, the people destroyed in the flood, and all the ungodly, innocent, not guilty, and forgiven of all sin and gave unto them the status of saints.[6]

Thesis 3 is perhaps the least offensive, although in its context it is thoroughly misleading. Thesis 1 confuses "objective" and "subjective" justification by saying of the former what may only be said of the latter, namely that sinners have "received" forgiveness. Objective justification means that forgiveness has been *obtained* for and is being *offered* to all in the Gospel—not that anybody has "received" it. The *receiving* can happen only through faith, *sola fide*. Thesis 2, that after Christ's sacrifice "God regards all sinners as guilt-free saints" is simply false, St. Jn. 3:36; I Jn. 5:12. And Thesis 4 about hell's human denizens being pronounced innocent, given "the status of saints," etc. is fantasy. An unbiblical logic has driven biblical language senseless: what can it possibly mean to have (or, worse, *receive!*) "the status of saints" in hell? The grace and forgiveness which Christ obtained for all, had been offered to the dead during their life-time, in the means of grace (St. Lk. 16:29; Heb. 9:27), but are in no way given to the godless in hell, where there is no Gospel, hence no forgiveness *(Large Catechism,* Creed, 56).

The trouble with these repulsive "Kokomo" statements is that they ignore the pivotal significance of the means of grace and thereby abandon the proper distinction of Law and Gospel. That, too, in essence is what was wrong with Samuel Huber's proposal, early in the 17th century, of a notion of "universal justification," which was duly rejected by representative Lutherans at the time. The story is told in detail by Dr. Tom Hardt of Sweden, in the 1985 *Festschrift* for Robert Preus, *A Lively Legacy.*[7] Hardt is a meticulous scholar who demonstrates in detail the difference between the *wrong* sort of "objective justification," as taught by Huber, and the *right* sort, as found in C.F.W. Walther's Easter preaching and theology.

In light of Mr. Darby's citation of the late Dr. Siegbert Becker in support of the "Kokomo" theses *(HD,* p. 240), I now regret my editorial note *(A Lively legacy,* p. 78) which attempted to shield Becker against criticism by Hardt on justification. However *technically* defensible my cavils may have been, the larger truth signaled by the "Kokomo" affair is that Hardt was right and I was wrong.

(b) That God remains unchangeable, also in the Incarnation and the Redemption.

Pieper insists on this repeatedly, in connection with the Incarnation, for example when he argues that *kenoticism,* the notion that the Son of God gave up some divine attributes in His Incarnation, falls beneath the level even of the natural knowledge of God (II:223-224)!

When it comes to the Redemption, the simple but sublime words of St. John 3: 16 define the irreversible order: "God so loved the world that He gave His only-begotten Son." The antecedent divine Love motivates the satisfaction of His own justice, not *vice versa!*

It was Huber's bad theology which speculated about God's inner essence, and an alleged change there; for Walther objective justification meant "an external act of God, the Father raising His Son," thus "turning it toward the world" (Hardt, p. 66).

Pieper wrote that "a change of heart took place, not in men, but in God" (II:346). He meant the right thing, which was to safeguard the objectivity of the Redemption as an action taking place from God's side, not from man's, as the various subjective or "moral influence" theories of the atonement hold. Pieper's sense is clear from the technical term he employs, *"in foro divino"* [in the divine forum or tribunal]. This is what Pieper meant by God's "heart" here. But the language is unfortunate—as though there was a change in God's inmost being.

The great Wisconsin Synod dogmatician, A. Hoenecke used more careful language, expressly rejecting the notion of a change in God. The relevant biblical texts, he wrote, "say nothing of a reversal of the sensibility or state of mind [Umstimmung des Gemuets] of God, but only of certain arrangements, judicial facts and activities."[8] The reconciliation of II Cor. 5:19, he said, means not "a changed position of His heart" but a changed "relation" (Verhaeltnis) between God and the world.

(c) That the wrath of God did not simply cease with the death and resurrection of Christ.

This of course is a corollary of point (b), see *HD,* pp. 13,115, 248, and passim. God's reconciliation with the world, the cessation of His wrath, hence "forgiveness, life, and salvation" are an accomplished fact and reality—in Christ (I Jn. 5: 11, 12)! *Outside* of Christ and of the Gospel, God remains a "consuming Fire" (Deut. 4:24, Heb. 12:29). It is a matter of rightly distinguishing Law and Gospel:

"These are the two chief works of God in men, to terrify and to justify and quicken the terrified. One or the other of these works is spoken of throughout Scripture" *(Apology,* XII, 53). One is Law, which proclaims God's wrath over sin, and the other is the Gospel, which imparts mercy and forgiveness. "Since the beginning of the world these two proclamations have continually been set forth side by side in the church of God with the proper distinction" *(Formula of Concord,* SD, V, 23, compare 11-15).

(d) That a deterioration of conventional U.S. Lutheran theology has occurred in this century, such that the pervasive sentimentalism of popular culture blunts and blurs even the clear contours of the Law/Gospel distinction and of the pivotal position of the means of grace.

This formulation is of course my summary, not Mr. Darby's own language. But I do not think that I have misrepresented him. He writes, for example:

- Preaching is much less "Law" oriented.
- Preaching against sin is very general when it does exist.
- Outward peace and harmony are considered virtues *per se.*
- Sermons are focused on living the Christian life, rather than continual instruction in doctrinal truth.
- Our publications are focused on public relations and practical problem solving rather than explanation of doctrine.
- The Seminary curriculum is far more practical and far less doctrinal.

If the central Law-Gospel message of the Church has been blurred, the only message which has the power to solve all other problems, then could that explain why sin and error hold no terror for the vast majority of modern Lutherans? Could that explain why modern Lutherans are so apathetic toward the doctrinal aberrations that go on all around them? Could that explain why modern "conservative" Lutherans participate in things that they were taught (as children) were sin and error? Are modern Lutherans overcoming their guilty conscience with some "comforting" justification such as: "Well, all sins are forgiven, so that includes these sins also"? (HD, p. 3).

Consider for example the fast growing Church Growth Movement in the "conservative" Lutheran church bodies. What message do you think they are proclaiming to get all those people in their doors?

- Do you think the unchurched baby-boomers are hearing God's LAW and WRATH above the guitar music?
- Do you think the "me generation" keeps packing the mega-churches even though "Pastor Bob" specifically condemns *their* pet sins, sins like worldliness, coveting, gambling, lust and drunkenness?

• Do you think that Church Growth Enthusiasts, focused on meeting the *felt needs* of their audience, are teaching that *any* willful, persistent sin expels saving faith?

Whether one likes the change or not, most honest Lutherans will admit that the *de facto* leading message of modern Lutheranism is "you are already forgiven" (p. 15).

And by breeding carnal security and neglect of the means of grace, the modern version of objective justification weakened the love of doctrine everywhere it spread (p. 178).

The decades following World War I marked a critical transition for the Missouri Synod, as it tried hard to escape its "German" image. By giving up the German language in the church, we effectively jettisoned our tremendous literary heritage, not least of which was Luther's Bible, which had served orthodox Lutheranism for so long. Exciting dialogs now become possible with other church bodies (p. 178n).

The omission of the means of grace from this teaching shows that Rev. *NN,* like his mentors, may have drunk deeply from Reformed waters.

The Forgotten Efficacy and Sufficiency of the Means of Grace

The all important question is still this: when did the means of grace lose their efficacy and sufficiency to overcome the doubts that Christians occasionally experience? Are the means of grace the only solution to the problem? And what about the situation where our "weak and faltering faith" results from willful, persistent sin which destroys saving faith? Do we Christians live a life of daily repentance (contrition brought on by the Law and faith renewed/strengthened by the Gospel) or do we anesthetize our consciences by repeating the mantra "God has already forgiven the whole world, and I am certainly included in that"? Rev. *NN's* teaching actually diverts people away from what is distinctly Lutheran:

• Ongoing confession;
• The efficacy and sufficiency of God's words;
• The means of grace (pp. 235-236).

The new generation had a different vision of the Missouri Synod that could be summarized as follows: "We already have the pure doctrine, now let us go out there [and] be EFFECTIVE!" This new generation of churchmen proved again and again their willingness to adjust or downplay doctrine to reach that goal. The modern version of objective justification also met the ecumenical spirit of the age because ... at least we could agree with other churches that everybody is already forgiven. And after all, was not that enough in order to have church fellowship? ...

Anyone who has ever tried to speak the words of God to an impenitent sinner knows that "you're already forgiven" goes over a lot better than "you're a wretched sinner road to hell." ...

When sin in our life troubles our conscience, when spiritual doubts arise in our hearts because of "pet" sins, what do we do? No other question has more urgency for the professing Christian. This is where the rubber meets the road in the life of a Christian. Does this weak faith, troubled conscience and spiritual doubt drive us deeper into the words of God, which then drive us to contrition, confession and faith-strengthening absolution? Or do we anesthetize our conscience by repeating the mantra of objective justification: *"All sins are already forgiven . . . even Judas' in hell . . . so that certainly includes this sin of mine that I do not really want to give up"?* . . .

I encourage you to test the widespread acceptance of this doctrine for yourself: ask fellow professing Lutherans what they "do" when spiritual doubts arise. See if they talk about the means of grace, word and Sacrament, or the "fact" that all sins are already forgiven. Ask them what they "do" when they find themselves stuck in a particular sin ... see whether their answer includes contrition, confession and absolution (pp. 251-252).

These are very astute and relevant observations. Given the self-indulgent outlook of the times, the "Kokomo" views are just the twisted sort of version of objective justification one would expect to arise. The undercutting of the means of grace is its chief theological flaw and spiritual peril. That is also why the ex-Calvinist Samuel Huber's version of "universal justification" was rejected by orthodox Lutherans at the time (see references to Tom Hardt's essay above). It appears that Mr. Darby's entire work on the subject is motivated by his strong conviction that the "Kokomo" approach is inimical to faith and spiritual life as understood and confessed by the Lutheran Church. This conviction is not to be gainsaid. All criticism of Mr. Darby's work, to be fair, ought to start with this basic acknowledgment.

One need not agree with all of Hermann Sasse's criticisms of Missouri Synod theology and its 17th century Orthodox roots—I for one do not—in order to recognize the deep significance of his trenchant lament: **"The Lutheran Confessions no longer play the role in the life and in the theological thinking of the Missouri Synod, in fact, of all of American Lutheranism by far which they played during the 19th century."** [9]

The reason for this fateful weakening of the Confessional paradigm in Lutheran theological thinking must be sought not in fanciful conspiracies but simply in the process of "acculturation" to the North American environment—which also helps to explain such conspiracies as no doubt did arise! Although Mr. Darby's work seems to make much of the conspiratorial factor, he adds this sensible explanation: "I do not suggest this was a conspiracy *of men* stretching over 100 years, but rather a conspiracy of our real enemy, Satan, who is capable of using even small openings to introduce error into the once-orthodox Synodical Conference" *(HD,* p. 118). Fair enough.

That the *sacramental* dimension of Lutheran faith and piety is most at risk in this "acculturation" seems fairly obvious. There was not much of that in the English-language literature which filled the void of the lost

German staples. Somewhere among my papers there is a little devotional booklet issued in the 1940's by the Missouri Synod's Army and Navy Board, as it was then called. The booklet offers various prayers, but not the morning, evening, and mealtime prayers from the Catechism. I do not recall whether there is a form for emergency baptism. There is, however, a model prayer for "receiving the Lord Jesus" into one's heart!

Not to be discounted in the acculturating distortion of "objective justification" is the pervasive influence of Schleiermacher and his multitude of followers. Hoenecke put it like this:

> According to Schleiermacher there is only a universal *[allgemeinen]* eternal decision *[Ratschluss]* of justification, which in turn is nothing else than the decision to send Christ, and in the end is nothing else than the decision to create the human race, insofar, that is, as only in Christ is human nature completed. In the decision of the Redemption is implied *[liegt,* lies] according to Schleiermacher already that mankind *[die Menschen]* are pleasing to God in His Son; there is no need for an individual temporal act of justification upon each individual *[einzelnen]* human being. It is necessary only that the individual human being become aware of this, that in God's decision of the Redemption in Christ he has already been justified and made pleasing to God (ID:355, my translation).

Cultural sentimentalism, the anti-sacramental "spirituality" of Reformed sectarianism, and the individualist-experiential bent of "respectable" theology in the wake of Schleiermacher, make up a potent brew, which-as Mr. Darby is quite right to point out-poses a formidable threat in our time and place to the right understanding *(Augsburg Confession* VII!) of justification and the means of grace. '

5. Indefensible Theses of Mr. Larry Darby:

(e) That there was "no distinct, divine judicial act around A.D. 30" *(HD,* p. 75).

This is one of the core components of Mr. Darby's opposition to what he regards as the "new" and unacceptable version of objective justification. The basic logic is that God foreknew everything from eternity, that both His grace and His wrath are unchangeable, and that the eternal election has already determined the outcome. Therefore there can be "no distinct, divine judicial act around A.D. 30."

When Mr. Darby concedes the terminology "objective reconciliation" or even "objective justification" he means no more by it than "the fact that God has always regarded mankind with grace (in addition to His burning wrath)" (HD, p. 131). The Law had been

> fulfilling its condemnatory function long before A.D. 30. The Law came along, so to speak, found this Man hanging on the cross on Whom

lay the sins of the world, and it automatically subjected Him to the torments of hell, with the full foreknowledge and approval of the Father. No distinct judicial act was required to understand this matter, and since Scripture does not teach such an act, neither should we (p. 195).

The same goes for the Resurrection: It "can be seen quite scripturally as the natural outcome of the fact that the Law had finished its work upon Him ... No distinct judicial act was involved" (p. 195). Again: "We equate *objective justification* with Christ's procurement of forgiveness for all men. This 'transaction' took place in the mind of God before the foundation of the world. We must not assert that there was a distinct, judicial act around A.D. 30 since that cannot be proved from Scripture" (p. 216).

Mr. Darby is grappling with a real conundrum: the eternal, unchangeable God acting in time, in human history. There is no logical, philosophical solution to this "problem." Both paradoxical aspects must be fully maintained, as Scripture does, and neither may be sacrificed to the other. Yes, God foresaw everything, but this does not mean that He never does anything new: the creation happened in time, not in eternity; the Incarnation happened in time, not in eternity, and so did the Redemption and all other facets of Our Lord's divine-human, high priestly work of salvation. If there can be no distinct divine acts (why should only "judicial" ones be forbidden?) in time, then the creation and the Incarnation did not happen either.

Furthermore, if there can be no new "distinct judicial" acts, then what happens in personal justification through faith? When the ungodly person's "faith is counted for righteousness" to him by God (Rom. 4:5), that is certainly a "distinct, divine judicial act." There have been millions of such divine judicial acts in history. If God's eternal foreknowledge does not forbid these millions of judicial acts, why should it forbid the one great world-embracing judicial act in the Cross and Resurrection, which is the real and objective basis for all the millions of individual "applicatory" judicial acts? Justification is by definition a judicial act.

As Hoenecke pointed out (see point 4b above}, the specifying phrases in II Cor. 5:18-21, "not imputing trespasses," "made Him to be sin," describe not changes within God, but "only ...certain arrangements, judicial facts and activities," such that they "alter" the "relationship between God and [the world]" *(Dogmatik,* ID:191)— in other words, "distinct judicial act[s] around A.D. 30."

It is worth quoting here Pieper's reply to the modern sentimentalists' complaint that the notion of God's reconciliation of the world with Himself through Christ's substitutionary satisfaction is too "juridical" and not sufficiently "ethical." To avoid the imprecise and lackluster prose of the English version, I have translated the following from Pieper's German *Dogmatik* (II 420-421, a passage which Mr. Darby unfortunately omits from his detailed treatment of Pieper):

Answer: That can hardly be changed if we want to abide by Scrip-

84

ture. According to Scripture, as it happens, the process of world-reconciliation is in *all its* factors juridical. Of a decidedly juridical kind and nature is God's law, in that it demands from men a perfect obedience, Matt. 22:37 ff. Unadulteratedly juridical is also the curse of the law, which extends over the transgressors of the law. Gal 3:10. Purely juridical is the placement of Christ under the law given to men, Gal. 4:4,5, since Christ for His own Person stood *above* the law, Mat 12:8. Purely juridical is the divine transfer of human guilt and punishment upon Christ, since God made Him to be sin, Who for His own Person knew of no sin, 2 Cor. 5:21. Purely juridical is the execution of punishment upon Christ since Christ had for His Person deserved no punishment, but in Him the Righteous suffered for the unrighteous, I Pet 3:18. Purely juridical or an unadulterated actus *forensis* is the divine action whereby God then when He reconciled the world with Himself, did not impute to men their sin..., 2 Cor. 5:19, and whereby through the Righteousness of the *one* Christ came to justification of life for all men, Rom. 5:18. Of a purely juridical kind therefore is also "the *word* of reconciliation" (...2 Cor. 5:19), that is of the reconciliation *already effected* through Christ, which makes known grace or the divine forgiveness of sins among all nations (Lk. 24:47) and awaits only acceptance *through faith.* In the purely juridical character of the Gospel, which proclaims grace or forgiveness of sins, lies the reason for the fact that the Gospel *works faith* in man (Rom 10:17) and that man is *subjectively justified* before God *out of* faith (sola fide), without any righteousness of his *own* (...Phil. 3:9). On these purely juridical occurrences–so Scripture instructs us further–rests now also all *human ethics,* about which the combatants against the juridical notion of world-reconciliation are so concerned (all emphases in original).

This excerpt, incidentally, shows how skillfully Pieper weaves actual biblical language into his argument–and how difficult therefore it is to translate his text without loss of subtle nuance and precision. I hope, too, that we shall not have to quibble about the different terms "judicial," "juridical," and "forensic," all of which mean the same thing in this context. Being equivalent to the German "richterlich."

The truly cosmic (Col. 1:20) change in our standing before God, though of course seen and willed by Him from eternity, was in fact brought about by the life, death, and Resurrection of Christ, and therefore in history and in time— not "once upon a time," but "once for all" (Rom. 6:10, Heb. 7:27, 9:12, 10:10) Therefore also we have in Him a *new,* and *better,* and *permanent* Testament (II Cor. 3:6-18, and all of Hebrews).

It is a pity that for his treatment of the time/eternity paradox in Pieper, Mr. Darby [HD, pp. 131-134] chose to repair to the first volume of *Christliche Dogmatik,* and to by-pass the relevant discussion in volume two. I quote from the long footnote #1041 against Ihmels (pp. 438-439):

So we must maintain on the one hand on the basis of Scripture, that the decision to reconcile the world [Ratschluss der Weltversoehnung] through Christ belongs to *eternity*, which is unchangeable; on the other hand Scripture leads us to think of a change of attitude [Umstimmung] of God or a transformation [Umwandlung] of His wrath into grace, which has been *effected* [bewirkt] through Christ's doing and suffering in the fullness of time 1900 years ago. Condescending to our human powers of comprehension Scripture presents the matter thus: *At that [past] time* [damals], when the Righteous One suffered and died for the unrighteous, we were reconciled with God through the death of His Son. *At that time,* when Christ was put under God's law given to men and when He fulfilled it in the place of men, justification of life came about for all men through the *one* Righteousness. *At that time,* when God through Christ reconciled the world to Himself, He (God) did not impute their sin to the world of men, that means, *with Himself* [bei sich], "before His tribunal." He let *grace* towards the world of men take the place of *wrath.* Whoever now, like Ihmels, while invoking the immutability of God, calls these thoughts "misleading,"... thereby renounces *Scriptural* [schriftgemaesse] thoughts of the Redemption, which has taken place through Christ *in the fullness of time* (my translation; all emphases in original).

As for God's *election of grace,* it is quite out of place as an argument against universal justification (see *HD,* pp 49-54, 209, passim). As Pieper points out, "in Scripture the doctrine of the election of grace is given not a *central* but an *auxiliary* position. It serves the presentation of the *sola gratia" (Christliche Dogmatik* III 535, my translation). Citing the very language from *Formula of Concord* XI to which Darby appeals in *HD,* p. 53, Pieper says: "Also the Lutheran Confession defines as purpose of the doctrine of election the confirmation of the *sola gratia"* (p. 556) And in II:497 Pieper had already pointed out that even in Rom. 9-11 St. Paul treats election "not as a central article, but as *an auxiliary article to the doctrine of grace,"* and that the Apostle opposes the election of grace *"not* to gratia universalis [universal grace], but to liberum arbitrium (free will]."

To marshal election against objective justification is really to direct it against universal grace. Although Mr. Darby wishes to maintain universal grace in obedience to I Tim. 2:4 *(HD,* p. 49), his foreknowledge/election logic relentlessly gets in the way. So at p. 82 he accepts that the Holy Spirit is "willing to work all this in every one who hears the Gospel" but objects to the (1991 Catechism) wording that He "earnestly wants to convert all people and bring them to salvation through the Gospel." Is the universal grace of the Gospel then not *serious* grace, or is that Gospel not seriously offered to all mankind? One should read Pieper's spirited defense of universal and serious grace—and even the English of *Christian Dogmatics* III:21-34 is quite clear and explicit enough on these crucial matters, to which he returns again and again in the rest of his work.

On p. 50 Mr. Darby makes this remarkable assertion: "Stoeckhardt is also right to reject the error that *'As a consequence of reconciliation God pursues sinners further, calls them through the Gospel, and seeks to effect their conversion.'* This error clearly contradicts the perfect foreknowledge of God, His election, and His immutability." Despite the professions of universal redemption and reconciliation that follow, the appeal to foreknowledge, election and immutability here makes sense only if directed against universal grace, that is, God pursuing sinners with the Gospel, seeking to convert them.

The trouble is that our author has clearly misunderstood Stoeckhardt's intention. [10] Stoeckhardt was refuting the views of "positive" 19th century theologians like Thomasius and Luthardt, who downgraded world-reconciliation to forgiveness (=justification) as a mere possibility rather than an actual fact and reality. What Darby regards as too strong, saying too much, Stoeckhardt rejects as too weak, saying far too little. Stoeckhardt attacks the "positive" crowd of theologians not for saying that God pursues sinners with the Gospel but for making that Gospel far too iffy and in need of completion by human responses—as though faith had to establish and bring about forgiveness rather than merely receive and accept it.

(f) That the Resurrection of Christ was only one absolution among others, not THE absolution of the world *(HD,* pp. 101,105, 113-114, etc.).

The devaluation of the resurrection here becomes downright offensive. "Pieper and Walther were willing to speak about the event of the resurrection as one actual absolution, never suggesting that it was anything more than a reminder of the first one spoken in the Garden of Eden. However, the English version speaks of this event as if it were the *only* absolution, as if it proves that God had just completed a divine judicial act" (p. 101). Easter only "one actual absolution" among others? Nothing "more than a reminder [!] of the first one spoken in the Garden of Eden"? If this were really Pieper's original sense, then the English translation must be regarded as a vast improvement! Nor is this a casual slip in *HD* We read again on p. 114:

> Pieper's use of "a" reminds us that Christ's resurrection was not a unique event in time in regard to the way God regards sinful mankind, or a signal of a *change* in God. Similar absolutions have been spoken since the time of the Fall in the Garden of Eden. The English translators' change to "the" implies that *this event* in time proves a change in God and the status of mankind brought about by a distinct, divine judicial act around A.D. 30.

A footnote on the same page adds the final indignity: "As a brief reminder of the proper application of Absolution, we also note that the manifestation of this particular Absolution (i.e. the resurrection) was *only* to Christ's disciples, not to the impenitent." So now the Resurrection becomes if not quite "a" private, then at least "a" semi-secret absolution! *HD* even criticizes "the teaching of universal objective justification" for "revolv[ing] around the resurrection as the pivotal point *in time* in the process of salvation..." (p. 101)

This flies in the face of the whole New Testament economy of salvation, which culminates precisely in the Resurrection of our divine-human Redeemer. See the wealth of material in section 3 above. Given the centrality of the Resurrection as the founding fact of Christianity (Acts 17:30, 31; I Cor. 15!), which is celebrated therefore not just once a year but every week, on the "First" or "Lord's" Day (St. John 20:19-29; Acts 20:7; Rev. 1:10), it cannot possibly be just one of many items *in any list!* In 1893 Pieper put it like this, on behalf of the entire Synodical Conference:

> With our sins upon him Christ entered into the prison-house of death, absolved from *our* sins he was set free in his resurrection. Hence it is seen that the resurrection of Christ actually involves an absolution of the whole world, and the absolution we pronounce is nothing but a repetition or echo of what God has long since pronounced. [11]

If there is any "echoing" to be done, then by other things "echoing" the resurrection — never the other way round! This also explains what is meant elsewhere by saying that the Resurrection was a "factual" [tatsaechliche) absolution. The implied contrast is not "fictitious" or anything like that, but simply "verbal." Unlike all the absolutions in *words,* from Genesis to Revelation, and in the church from Pentecost till the end of days, the resurrection is absolution in the form of FACT or DEED, that unique culminating fact, fount, and source out of which all *verbal* absolutions flow. Like Caiaphas before him (St. John 11:49-52), little did Rudolf Bultmann realize the true sense of his famous phrase that "Jesus is risen into the Gospel"! And of that, Holy Absolution is the concentrate.

It follows that the argument from the difference between the indefinite article in Pieper's original German ["a factual absolution"] and the definite article in the English translation ["the actual absolution"] *(HD,* pp. 113-114) is an illusion. Although both English and German have definite and indefinite articles, the usage is not identical. Often, for instance, the definite article is natural in a German phrase, but unnatural in English (e.g., "Eindruck der Wirklichkeit" [Pieper II:436] must go into English without the article, as "impression of reality." It cannot possibly be "impression of *the* reality" unless there were a further specification of the term, such as "impression of the reality of the transaction"). Although I am not a German language expert, I would venture to say that sometimes the indefinite article is used in preference to the definite *for the purpose of stressing the qualitative content of the assertion.* Such usage would parallel the omission of the definite article in Greek constructions like St. John 1:1. Here the lack of the definite article before "God" means not that "the Word was a god," as Jehovah's Witnesses maintain fraudulently, but precisely the opposite, that the very attribute of *divinity* is being stressed: "It was nothing short of *God* that the Word was."

No inference may be drawn therefore from the presence or absence of

articles against the uniqueness of the Resurrection as the factual absolution (=justification) of the world. The semantic content of the assertions, regardless of articles, dictates the meaning. For instance: "Not a
few regard the resurrection of Jesus Christ as no more than a beautiful
addition, a brilliant decoration of the real salvatory acts of the Redeemer
of the world, as a precious pearl in the crown of redemption, but not as
that very crown itself. They do not know what to do with it..." Nor is
there any hesitation to use the definite article when it fits. "That the resurrection of Christ is the [die] fully valid justification of all men" (Both
examples are from C. F. W Walther, quoted by Hardt, pp. 62 and 73, note
56, and 61 and 73, note 51, respectively. My emphases).

(g) That only actual biblical words and expressions carry full divine, spiritual power.

Warnings against human theological reconstructions of Holy Scripture
("The Efficacy and Sufficiency of God's Words." *HD,* pp. 7-10) are certainly in order, especially nowadays when the sacred text is so often made
to fit fashionable concerns like "gender-neutral language." Yet the term
"God's Words" seems to be restricted unduly to verbatim biblical citations
– everything else being "human" words and explanations. This point is
driven to the extreme in the correspondence with Pastor Rolf Preus.

> The *real* issue is whether there is something fundamentally unfaith-
> ful about trying to convey spiritual truth with our words instead of
> God's explicit words. Man's words have often confused or deceived...
> But God's words have never deceived.
> -I believe that God's very words, preserved in Holy Scripture, say
> what they mean and mean what they say (what theologians like to
> call perspicuity)...
> -I believe that these very words alone have the power to convey
> truth — not just convey it to heads (knowledge and assent) but also
> to the heart and soul. This is what theologians like to call efficacy
> *(OJ,* p. 17)

By way of a first approach one should note that the biblicist anxiety
about exact inspired wordings is not a normal or natural part of Lutheran
piety. The Catechism, for instance — except in the Decalogue and the
Lord's Prayer — accustoms us to saying first a brief "human" summary
of what the thing is, or means, or gives, and then, if necessary, asking,
"Where is this written?" The devil tried to seduce the Lord with the *ip-
sissima verba,* the very words of God (St. Mt. 4.6) — so these can obviously be used deceitfully. Luther, on the other hand, habitually drove off
Satan not with biblical citations — nothing wrong with those of course
— but with sacramental defiance. "I am baptized!" Whereas Southern
Baptists would presumably direct troubled souls to specific Scripture-
texts, Lutherans direct them above all to the Absolution, and so to ecclesiastical, "human" wordings: "Upon this your confession I as a called and

ordained servant [Slavonie: 'His unworthy servant'] ... forgive you all your sins..." Also, the meaning of the Third Commandment bids us attend to "preaching and His Word." These are not two different things: the "and" is basically "epexegetical"— see the Latin version and the *Large Catechism.*

The underlying truth here is that of the "unity" of the Word of God (see Robert Preus, *The Inspiration of Scripture,* pp. 17 ff.). The divine *efficacy* attaches not to the "materia" (the [divinely chosen] letters and words in the human languages [Hebrew, Greek]) as such, but to the "forma," the divine meaning or sense, which can be re-stated — also translated! — in different words without loss of truth or power. Preus:

> The efficacy of the Word of God does not inhere in the letters and syllables and words as they are written. These are merely symbols, the vehicle *(vehiculum)* of the divine content, the *forma,* of the Word which alone is the Word of God, properly speaking. It is extremely important to bear in mind that the dogmaticians are never speaking of the Bible as a book, of the *materia* of Scripture, or of the *materia* of the Word of God in general, when they say that the Word of God is efficacious (p. 174).

The basic units of faith and theology are not so many biblical books as such [unlike the Roman and Reformed confessions, the Lutheran Book of Concord does not specify exactly how many books make up the canon], but the divinely revealed "articles" that make up the Christian "doctrine" (in the New Testament true Christian "doctrine" occurs only in the singular — as opposed to the plural "doctrines" of men and of demons):

> The first part of the Articles treats the sublime articles of the divine majesty...

> The first and chief article is this, that Jesus Christ, our God and Lord "was put to death for our trespasses and raised again for our justification," Rom. 4.

> The Word of God shall establish articles of faith and no one else, not even an angel *(Smalcald Articles* I; II/I/1; II/II/15).

> These articles of the Creed, therefore, divide and distinguish us Christians from all other people on earth *(Large Catechism,* Creed, 66).

> ... agreed in the doctrine and in all its articles ... *(Formula of Concord,* SD, X. 31).

Exact biblical wording is crucial of course in determining the right content or doctrine — but it is that content or doctrine which for Luther is always the essential thing.

90

"Could you please show me," writes Mr. Darby, "where the Bible describes itself as a 'body of Christian doctrine' or 'living organism'?"

Well, there is first of all the "one faith" (Eph. 4:5, compare Jude 3). Then there is the one "doctrine" or even "pattern of doctrine" of Christ and the Apostles (St. John 7:16; Acts 2:42; Rom. 6:17; 16:17. I Tim 4:16; Tit. 1:9, II John 9, etc.). Thirdly, there is the liberating truth, Word of truth. etc. (St. John 8:32: 17:17: Eph. 1:13; 4:21; II Tim. 2:15). Fourthly, there is the one and life-giving Word or Gospel (St. Mk. 1:1, Acts 15:7, Rom. 1:16, I Cor. 15:1, Gal. 1:6-9; Phil. 1:7, II Tim. 1:10, Heb. 4:12, I Pet. 1:23-25). All these expressions imply not disjointed [*articulus* means "joint" or "member" of an organism in Latin] bits and pieces, but one grand revealed unity, the "mystery" of salvation (Col. 1:26-27, 2:2-3, 4:3, I Tim 3:16), its unifying, ordering Centre being the God-Man Himself (St. John 5:39, I Cor. 3:11, Eph. 2:20). The *mysteries* [plural, as in I Cor. 4:1] are the various particular aspects ["articles"] of the one saving truth—including the "sacraments" (=Latin for "mysteries:" see *Apology,* XXIV, 80). Here is a case where later ecclesiastical usage ["sacrament"] is much narrower than the biblical ["mystery"]. But, properly explained, this does not change the doctrine.

It is difficult to know what to make of Mr. Darby's argument from, among other things, "Exegesis, rather than doctrine, is the main topic of discussion among pastors and teachers" to the conclusion "in short, we have lost our zeal for God's very words" *(HD,* p. 3). It would seem that "zeal for God's very words" would impel one precisely *towards* exegesis, which occupies itself with "God's very words" in the original languages. Yet Mr. Darby is right, I think, in sensing that something has gone awry in the turn *from* doctrine (content!) to "exegesis" (method). Ideally sound content and sound method go together.

Mr. Darby's underlying claim here is that "objective justification" is a human theological construct which lacks support in the "pattern of healthy words" (II Tim 1:13), that is, in express biblical texts. The *major* premise is of course sound. Whatever cannot be proved from explicit biblical texts, may not be given out as Christian doctrine or teaching *Quod non est biblicum non est theologicum.* Whatever is not biblical is not theological either. That is axiomatic. What is not sound is the *minor* premise, that "objective justification", in fact, lacks the proper basis in express biblical texts. In addition to all the material already presented above, I urge close attention here to just a few concrete biblical specifics.

(1) The world's Redeemer is said to have been "justified" (I Tim. 3:16) —obviously in the Resurrection. Since as Lamb of God He had no sins of His own, but only the world's, it is clear that somehow the world was "justified" in Him when He was "justified."

(2) In Eph. 1:7 and Col. 1:14 "redemption" and "forgiveness" are identified but of course forgiveness = justification (Rom 4:4-8).

(3) II Cor. 5.19 literally says that "God was, in Christ, reconciling the

91

world to Himself, not imputing to them their trespasses." The object of this non-imputation (=forgiveness=justification) was "the world," not any subset of it.

(4) Although, N.D. p. 29, tries to contrast three different translations of Rom. 5:18, the differences prove to be purely verbal. In content all three say exactly the same thing. Since the verse contains no verb, one has to be supplied. Luther's translation [which *ND* labels that of "Prof. Schmidt"] adds fewer words than the Authorized Version, and is thus more literal: "As now through the sin of one condemnation has come upon all men, so also through the righteousness of one justification of life has come upon all men." Verbatim, "justification" [which lead to life] is connected here with "all men." Of all verbs that might be supplied, "come upon" seems to be the most neutral or minimal or the least intrusive. But what does the text mean? Much useless quarreling can be avoided by paying heed to the wise and modest explanation printed by Walther in 1871: "Both acts [Adam's and Christ's] have an equally general signification and validity. But as not all men are personally condemned, although the 'judgment came upon all men to condemnation,' so not all men are really and personally justified, although the justification has through Christ's act 'come upon all men' " (quoted in Hardt, pp. 65 and 75, note 67). As condemnation is objectively "there" for all in Adam. Yet not everyone ends up actually condemned. So justification leading to life is "there" for all in Christ, even though not everyone ends up actually justified. And that is just what the distinction between "objective" and "subjective" justification is meant to express. Anything further (e.g. "Kokomo") is of evil.

At the very least all this shows that there is a proper basis in actual biblical language for the "objective/subjective," or better "universal/individual," distinction with reference to justification. It is not true, therefore, that the "justification" terminology is used in Scripture so narrowly and exclusively of the personal imputation of righteousness through faith that no other, broader use of the terms is permissible. In normal usage, both biblical and ecclesiastical, "justification" includes the personal appropriation through faith. There is biblical warrant, however for using that language also in the special sense of forgiveness as it has been acquired by Christ once and for all and is offered to all in the Gospel.

Even if "objective justification" could be rightly understood, asks Larry Darby, "what good is it?" *(HD,* pp. 36-39). He argues that the various errors against which "objective justification" has been asserted can be met better and more directly from Scripture without this artificial "theological construction." The fact is, however, that far from being some abstract "construction," the real point and thrust of the term and teaching is none other than to safeguard the fullness of salvation as it has been given to the world in Christ. Roman Catholicism denies the *intensive* perfection of Christ's reconciling work. According to the scheme of the Council of Trent, He earned for us not forgiveness and salvation as an outright gift, but only the opportunity to earn them with the aid of divine 'grace'! Calvinism, on the other hand, denies the *extensive* perfection of His saving work. Yes, says Geneva, Christ has done everything for our salvation, but not for everyone, only for the elect. The Wittenberg Reformation *alone* remains faithful to Scripture by teaching both the *intensive* and the *extensive* perfection of the Savior's accomplished work — and that is what "objective, universal justification" is meant to express.

Mr. Darby is quite right, as we have seen, to denounce a simplistic, "Kokomo"-style "comfort" that "since all people are forgiven, even Judas in hell, I am certainly included" (p. 37). Given Judas' actual fate it is difficult to detect any comfort in this sentiment. But that only by the way. Mr. Darby rightly argues that Christians should be pointed to the means of grace, not to the alleged sainthood of Judas. It is just here, however, that "universal justification" is so indispensable: without it, there can be no objective, reliable means of grace at all! The logic is not, "I am forgiven because all are forgiven," but: "I can rely on forgiveness in the Gospel and Sacraments, because it is there for all." If forgiveness did not exist in Christ and His Gospel objectively for all mankind, how could I possibly presume to think that I receive it in the means of grace? I would then, as in Calvinism, need more information about my election, by "experiencing" the Holy Spirit in my heart (!), before I could know whether the Gospel applied to me. That way lies a tragic return to the pre-Reformation *"monstrum incertitudinis"* (monster of uncertainty). A few samples will show the real means-of-grace rationale of "objective justification":

A. HOENECKE: "The underscoring of the universal justification is necessary in order to preserve the real content of the Gospel" *(Dogmatik* III:355; my translation).

C.F.W. WALTHER: "What now is actually the doctrine on which — to put it that way — absolution rests? We Lutherans teach about this briefly the following:

1. That Christ, the Son of God, took all sins of all sinners upon Himself and let them be imputed to Himself as if they were His own hence John the Baptist, pointing to Christ with his finger, says: 'Behold, this is God's Lamb, which bears the world's sin.' We teach:
2. That Christ by His poor, wretched life, by His suffering, by His crucifixion, by His dying has wiped out all people's sin and won (erworben) forgiveness of the same. No human being in the world is excepted, from Adam on down to the last (person) to be born into this world. For St. Paul writes 2 Cor. 5:21... And already Isaiah says, Is 53:5... We teach:
3. That God the Father has... by the Raising of Christ publicly attested before heaven and earth, before angels and men: 'This my beloved Son cried out from the Cross: "It is finished!" — and I declare hereby: Yes, it is finished [vollbracht, accomplished]! You sinners are redeemed! Here is forgiveness of sins for every one! It is already there!...' We teach:
4. That Christ, in commanding that the Gospel be preached to every creature, has thereby simultaneously commanded to preach forgive-

ness of sins to all men ... 'Oh, everything has already happened! Nothing more is to be done. You have only to believe what has happened, then you are helped.' We teach:

5. That Christ did not only in general command His apostles and those who were to succeed them in office to preach the Gospel, thus the forgiveness of sins, but also to speak the consolation to every single [one] who asks it of them: 'You are reconciled with God!' For if the forgiveness of sins has been won for all, then it has been won also for everyone individually... We teach:

6. That because now the forgiveness of sins, as already noted, has been won, not only the preacher in a special commission can proclaim it, but also every Christian man, also every Christian woman, yes, every child .... the issue is not 'what can the person [do]?' but: 'what has happened through Christ?'" (Die rechte Untersheidung von Gesetz und Evangelium [1901], pp. 158-159. For the sake of precision, I have given as literal a translation as I could. The English version of Law and Gospel [1929] is not exact enough for our purposes. It also gratuitously introduces that bloodless word "plan," beloved of Calvinists [see Pieper, Dogmatics III:247-248], in point 2 above. And in point 6 Walther's original sense regarding the "special commission" is not correctly reproduced).

F. PIEPER: "In the presentation of the doctrine of the means of grace one must stand with the *universal objective reconciliation* or justification. So we find it in the Scripture ... With the denial of the *gratia universalis* there disappear, consistently, also the means of grace" *(Dogmatik* III:123, 141; my translation).

"It should be borne in mind that God has already *absolved* the whole world in laying the sins of the whole world on Christ and in raising up Christ from the dead. With *our* sins upon him Christ entered into the prison-house of death, absolved from *our* sins he was set free in his resurrection. Hence it is seen that the resurrection of Christ actually involves an absolution of the whole world, and the absolution we pronounce is nothing but a repetition or echo of what God has long since pronounced ... Faith, indeed, is necessary on the part of man; not, however, to render God fully propitious, ... but to *accept* of [sic] the forgiveness already earned by Christ and now offered in the Gospel... It is of great importance to maintain this true conception of the Gospel, viz., that forgiveness of sins exists for every sinner before his conversion and faith for, how could man obtain forgiveness of sin *by faith, i.e.,* by *laying hold on it* by faith, if this forgiveness did not actually exist for him in Christ and were not offered to him in the Gospel? ... Absolution is founded on two facts, first, that God is perfectly reconciled through Christ to every sinner, secondly, that God has commanded this Gospel to be preached in the world .... Christ has already perfectly *acquired* forgiveness of sins for all men, and this forgiveness is offered and exhibited to men through the means of grace, to wit the Gospel and the Sacraments *(Distinctive Doctrines,* pp. 147-148, 150, 151).

(h) That the objective/subjective justification distinction is an unnecessary and misleading novelty, which Pieper's German *Christiliche Dogmatik* tolerated ["condone(d),"HD, p. 100)] and explained in an orthodox sense, but which the English translation [*Christian Dogmatics*] and the Missouri Synod's Catechism of 1991 materially falsified in the direction of the "Kokomo" excesses.

The 1872 Synodical Conference Essay and "Prof. Schmidt"

In my translation of this essay, which I entitled *Justification-Objective and Subjective* (Ft. Wayne, Concordia Theological Seminary Press, 1982), I offered the conjecture that Prof. F. A. Schmidt was the author. I did this on the basis of consultation with "informed sources." The result, however, was no more than an "informed guess." Some have even suggested to me that Walther himself was the author.

Pieper commended the essay's treatment of objective justification without reservations *(Dogmatik* II:611, note 1420: *Dogmatics* II:508, note 12). If this essay really had been a devious attempt on the part of "Prof. Schmidt" to introduce "error" by means of "subterfuge" *(HD* 20 ff.), would not some prominent Missouri Synod theologian have noticed it and offered some hint of criticism or reservation somewhere? On the contrary, the essay stands as a monument of soundness and sagacity in doctrinal discourse.

Mr. Darby is quite right to note that my translation and publication of the essay occurred at a time when this very matter was being debated again in our circles *(HD.* pp 19-20). My aim, to mix metaphors, was not to fan the flames but to calm the troubled waters by offering what I regarded as a truly balanced, moderate (in the good sense!), and responsible treatment of the subject. Hence my choice of title. It seemed to me that in our own discussions at the time, the topic was being distorted (as that of the ministry is today) by over-statements and over-reactions. The judicious, painstaking treatment in that first Synodical Conference Convention essay seemed — and still seems — to me to supply an ideal antidote and a sound traditional model or *modus docendi* (mode of teaching).

Roots in Lutheran Orthodoxy, Not "Made in America"

Mr. Darby himself recognizes that objective justification "has deeper roots than 1872" *(OJ,* p. 49). Only he is quite wrong in stating that "Adolph Hoenecke traced it to Schleiermacher." What Hoenecke traced to Schleiermacher was not the truth of objective justification—which he vigorously defended throughout — but a sentimental caricature and concern which eliminates the need for any actual, historical act(s) of justification (see p. 13 above). Pieper too complains of the "weakening of 'the historical work of Christ'" which "permeates the whole presentation of

95

the modern 'positive' theologians" *(Dogmatik* II:475, note 1096). Ironically therefore Mr. Darby's sustained polemic against a "judicial act around AD 30" sides with the Schleiermacher "positive" camp, not with orthodox Lutheran critics!

Our Synodical founding fathers consciously eschewed innovation. They were anxious to preserve dogmatic continuity with the orthodox church of earlier times. If they charitably corrected some weaknesses in the approaches of their illustrious predecessors, then not from newer, but from older, more genuine sources, Pieper quotes Walther as follows:

> Highly as we value the immense work done by the great Lutheran dogmaticians of [the 17th century], still they are not in reality the ones to whom we returned. We have returned above all, to our precious Concordia and to Luther. The dogmatic works of the 17th century, though storehouses of incalculably rich treasures of knowledge and experience, so that with joy and pleasure we profit from the day and night, are nevertheless neither our Bible nor our confession; rather, do we observe in them already a pollution of the stream that gushed forth in crystal purity in the sixteenth century *(Dogmatics* I:166).

The 1872 essay itself documented its continuity with standard-bearers like Quistorp, Gerhard, "Rohrberg" (which Hardt, p. 77, corrects to "Norborg") and others (my translation, pp. 21ff) Hoenecke was right: "Of universal justification our dogmaticians do not treat separately [besonders], but they do [treat of it] occasionally" *(Dogmatik* III:354).[12]

It is impossible to dispose of universal justification as a recent innovation.

Luther and Universal Justification

Darby *(HD,* pp. 29, 59, 61-63) is right in arging that Luther's usual interpretation of Rom. 5:18 is not that of Stoeckhardt, for instance. Tom Hardt's scholarship supports this conclusion (Hardt, pp. 68-69, note 11). To say only this, however, would be misleading in our context. Several qualifications must be spelled out:

First, Luther's actual *translation* (used but not invented by Prof. Schmidt," HD. P. 29) of Rom. 5:18 is that justification of life has come upon [ueber] all men."

Secondly, in his treatment of the references to Rom. 5:18 in the German St. Louis edition of Luther's works, even Dr. Hardt seems to have overlooked the following from a sermon for the Twelfth Sunday after Trinity (St. Louis edition, vol. XII, c. 850):

> So also St Paul speaks in Rom. 5,17,18, where he contrasts Adam and Christ. Adam, he says, was also a wellspring, who by his disobedience in paradise filled the world with sins and death, so that through the sin of this one [man] condemnation has come upon all men. Yet, again Christ with His obedience and righteousness has also become for us a Spring and Fullness, so that we also become righteous and

obedient out of it. And this Fullness is of such a nature that it runs much more richly and lavishly than the other one. For although by one sin of one man sin and death came [gegangen, went] upon all men, and the Law came in addition, through which sin became much mightier and stronger; but against that the grace and gift in Christ is so surpassingly rich and mighty, that it overflows and wipes out not only one sin of the one Adam (which had previously immersed all men into death), but all sin, so that now much rather those who receive the fullness of grace and gift (says he) to righteousness reign in life through the one Jesus Christ, etc.

Although the decisive importance of actual *reception* (by faith) is rightly stressed here, the surpassingly rich, objectively accomplished and fully existing Adam-antidote in Christ clearly covers "all sin," and is no less universal than Adam's poison — exactly the point of universal justification.

Thirdly, Luther teaches this universality explicitly:
He sent His Son into the world, heaped all the sins of all men upon Him, and said to Him:
"Be Peter the denier; Paul the persecutor, blasphemer, and assaulter; David the adulterer; the sinner who ate the apple in Paradise: the thief on the cross. In short, be the person of all men, the one who has committed the sins of all men. And see to it that You pay and make satisfaction for them.".... By this deed the whole world is purged and expiated from all sins, and thus it is set free from death and from every evil.
If the sins of the entire world are on that one man, Jesus Christ, then they are not on the world. But if they are not on Him, then they are still on the world. Not only my sins and yours, but the sins of the entire world, past, present, and future, attack Him, try to damn Him, and do in fact damn Him. Thus in Christ all sin is conquered, killed, and buried; and righteousness remains the victor and the ruler eternally *(Luther's Works,* vol. 26. pp. 280-281).

Fourthly, Luther expressly distinguishes forgiveness (which always equals justification) as won in Christ *then and there,* and as offered and given to our faith *here and now* in the Gospel:

We treat of the forgiveness of sins in two ways. First, how it is achieved and won. Second, how it is distributed and given to us. Christ has achieved it on the cross, it is true. But he has not distributed or given it on the cross. He has not won it in the supper or sacrament. There he has distributed and given it through the Word, as also in the gospel, where it is preached. He has won it once and for all on the cross. But the distribution takes place continuously, before and after from the beginning to the end of the world *(Luther's Works,* vol. 40. pp. 213-214).

St. Ambrose and the *Apology of the Augsburg Confession*

HD (pp. 25-28) makes much of the alleged "subterfuge" of the 1872 Synodical Conference essay in the way the citation from St. Ambrose in *Apology* IV:103 is handled. The citation is said to have been taken out of context, and wrongly to have attributed to the *Apology* as such what was only St. Ambrose's opinion. In addition, the translator is faulted for using the Tappert version rather than the *Triglotta*.

To start with the last point, Tappert was used simply because it is the most readable and accessible English version today. The original 1872 text followed the German of Mueller's edition. Tappert follows the Latin text of the *Apology,* which is the original for that document. Interestingly enough, the Latin original is even stronger than the German version used in 1872: According to the Latin, the Lord Jesus forgave "sin to all," whereas in German He forgave "sin to us."

The main complaint is that by ending the citation before the references to Baptism and faith, the false impression is created that Ambrose and the *Apology* were arguing for universal justification when in fact they were arguing for personal justification by faith, against works. But this is a total misunderstanding, as though to argue for the one were to argue against the other! On the contrary, every proper argument for justification by faith is an argument for the objective justification which it necessarily presupposes, and every argument for objective justification is an argument for justification by faith as its proper goal and conclusion. If justification indeed consists of the four constitutive elements the *Formula of Concord* (S.D. III:25) names, God's grace, Christ's merit, the Gospel, and faith, then an argument for point four can never be an argument against the first three! To argue for the one is to argue for the others. So our entire Lutheran dogmatical tradition has understood the matter — against Rome and Geneva, which take out or weaken this or that constituent element.

Further, it is fallacious to argue that the citation in question is being given only as an example of a Church Father's personal opinion. Clearly the *Apology* wholeheartedly endorses the Ambrosian citation, since the latter is taken to do more for the correct understanding of St. Paul than all the scholastics with their vain glorious titles (par. 105).

Finally, Mr. Darby does not seem to notice that his own citation (p. 27) from the *Triglotta* ("He took away the sin of the whole world") as "the real thing," does precisely what elsewhere he regards as forbidden: "you do not have the liberty to change Bible to past tense: ('Jesus *has taken away* the sin of the world.')" *(OJ,* p. 24).

C. F. W. Walther and Universal Justification

It is quite impossible to relegate Walther's consistent teaching of objective, universal justification to "[o]ne excerpt from an Easter Sermon — which was not even published until years later!" (OJ, p. 48). See

Hardt's scholarly work (cited earlier and appended to the present paper) for evidence of Walther's uniform and strongly expressed Easter theology of universal justification/absolution. Walther's enlarged edition of Baier's textbook, *Compendium Theologiae Positivae,* for instance, deliberately adds many orthodox testimonies to the universal justification in Christ (III:271-273). Also see the extended excerpts in Hardt (appended) from the 1860 Missouri Synod Convention essay on the relation between absolution and justification, and the 1871 *Lehre und Wehre* article on the dispute about objective justification. Walther was at the height of his powers and leadership then, and it is inconceivable that these essays would have appeared had they deviated from his theology.

It is fitting to cite in conclusion from the earlier (1878), shorter (only 13 theses) version of *Gesetz und Evangelium* (St. Louis. 1893), Walther's confession of objective justification, which at the same time warns against the very pitfalls which Mr. Darby's work is rightly intended to oppose. It is clear, however, that Walther's warning is not some sort of "qualification" to make a dubious "construction" seem plausible and acceptable! It is rather a case of rightly dividing Law and Gospel in presenting a central and indispensable truth, and demonstrates the real, proper, and intended meaning of "objective justification":

> So also it is with the doctrine of the *objective justification,* of the *objective reconciliation* and *redemption.* That is after all a surpassingly precious, delightful doctrine. It is a world full of comfort that lies in it. But this doctrine wants to be taught in such a way that the poor people don't get the idea: Christ has reconciled me, *now all is well [nun hat es gute Wege].* If you rightly underscore what an inexpressible comfort lies in this, that the redemption and reconciliation of the whole human race is an accomplished fact, that by the Raising of Christ all mankind was justified, then you must always add, that this has happened on the part of God but that in man something must first happen before it becomes his property. For if someone gives [schenkt] me something, that is still no proof that I have it. If I do not accept it, then it doesn't help me that it has been given to me. So it is also here. The dear God has gifted us all with what Christ has won for us, but only he who has come to faith has it, because only he has accepted it. *–Take heed to yourselves then, that you do not comfort falsely* (pp. 83-84; my translation, emphases in original).

Pieper in German and English

At the outset let me grant that the English version sometimes takes unwarranted liberties with the original German. In twenty years of teaching dogmatics from Pieper's volumes, I have noticed that students' misunderstandings and misgivings most often occur at points where the translators have improvised something that is not in Pieper's original German. For example, here is a point that arose in class only last week: *Dogmatics* [II:432 asserts: "Justifying faith is in every instance *fides ac-*

tualis, that is, the apprehension of the divine promises of the Gospel by an act of the intellect and will." But this directly contradicts p. 444: "It is a grave error to define faith as the conscious acceptance of the grace of God." It turns out that Pieper's original says nothing about "intellect and will," which imply something "conscious." It says rather: "Because faith, insofar as it puts [one] into possession of forgiveness, has for its *object* the promise of the Gospel, it is always fides *actualis,* that means, [an] *act* of grasping [Ergreifens, taking hold of], and that not only in the case of adults but also in that of children" *(Dogmatik* II:517; my translation).

The trouble is that Pieper's German original, though delightfully precise and expressive, abounds in the convoluted sentences typical of scholarly German syntax. English translations therefore must always break this prose up into shorter sentences, in order to achieve a readable English style. Clearly also Pieper's translators worked at a lower level of theological precision and comprehension than did the master. They "cut comers" and made the text more popular. Something was inevitably lost in the process. But that is all. There are no material — certainly no intentional — doctrinal changes or perversions evident in the translation, only clumsy infelicities of expression here and there. That applies also to the treatment of objective and subjective justification.

The wedge that *HD* attempts to drive between Pieper and Stoeckhardt, for instance, is entirely imaginary. Regarding the "universal or so-called objective justification" Pieper appeals without any reservations to Stoeckhardt's commentary on Romans and precisely to the pages *(Roemerbrief,* pp. 213 ff. and 262 ff.) which expound objective justification most strongly, on the basis of Rom. 4:25 and 5:18,19 (Pieper, *Dogmatik* II:612, note 1421).

The claim that Pieper only reluctantly "condoned" the term "objective justification" *(HD,* pp. 100, 128), is without merit or basis in fact, as even Mr. Darby's own citations show. We have already seen that the alternate uses of definite ("the") or indefinite ("a") articles here make no difference whatever. Incidentally, *all* references to objective justification in the original German index volume, under "Rechtfertigung," *include the definite article, i.e. "die objective Rechtfertigung."* And under "Auferstehung Christi" [Resurrection of Christ] the German index says: "Therefore the Resurrection THE factual [actual] absolution of the whole world of sinners, 2, 380, 412" (my translation and emphases). And there is nothing hesitant or concessive about statements like these:

The [reconciling] designates not a relation but a *doing,* and the immediately following [not imputing to them their trespasses] likewise designates a *doing:* God did not impute to men their sin. That means, He *justified* men [die Menschen], forgave them their sins (Rom. 4:6-8) = objective justification of the whole world of sinners *(Dogmatic* II:437, note 1040: my translation: emphases in original).

Charis designates of course the gracious disposition of God for Christ's sake, **favorem Dei**, the forgiveness of sins; justification, absolution [die Rechtfertigung, die Absolution]. Just so the proclaimed *eireinei* designates the objective peace which God has made with the world through Christ and [which He) makes known to the world as completed fact through the Gospel (II:475-476, note 1098).

It is futile to try to make anything else of this than the standard, traditional understanding objective justification. The effort to demonstrate doctrinal variance on the subject between Pieper's original and the translation, fails at all decisive points, when examined dispassionately. Some of the particulars (articles, resurrection, judicial act in time) have already been treated. The others also turn out to rest on misunderstanding or even self-contradiction:

- It is claimed that in German, though not in English, the term "so-called" has a "negative connotation" (HD, p. 104). No, it need not, but it can, and that in both English and German. For instance, when Hoenecke quotes Burk saying that "the relation of the universal justification to the otherwise so-called [sogenannten] justification can be expressed to the effect that it is just in the latter that the appropriation of the former occurs" (III:354-355; my translation), no, one can possibly hold that a "negative connotation" is being suggested here for the term "justification"! The same holds true for the Pieper-quotation in question: 6. dikaiosis; designates here the act of the divine justification, which took place through the act of the Raising of Christ from the dead, hence the so-called objective justification of the whole world of sinners. (Dogmatik II:380, my translation — note all the definite articles, as in original.). Pieper continues at once: "This is the truth of which especially Walther again emphatically reminded [people] in this country..." Pieper could not possibly have intended to put a negative connotation on a term designating a "truth" stressed by Walther!

- On the same Peiper-page the translators are said to have smuggled in the term "now," thus falsely introduc[ing] the element of time and change" (HD, p. 102). No, the error is in HD's version (p. 99), which skips the "now [nun]" which is in the original German, p. 380.

- On HD's pp. 102-103 the translators are blamed for the phrase "'reconciliation and justification,' as if these two terms were synonymous;" yet on p. 130 they are accused of "deliberate efforts ... to obscure" the fact that Pieper "equated objective reconciliation with objective justification"!

101

• HD, p. 156, claims that Pieper used "the term 'objective justification' guardedly" but "did not use subjective justification to describe what the Bible simply calls 'justification.'" Yet, on p. 134 just that use of "subjective justification" by Pieper (in the original German) is documented and noted.

• According to HD, p. 126, there is for Pieper "no meaningful sense in which everyone is 'justified.'" According to p. 128, Pieper "acknowledged that in this sense, there was 'a' justification before faith."

• On p. 136, HD rightly states that "both Pieper and [the 1872 essay] taught: 'in Christ God regards the world as righteous.'" But on pp. 32, 35, 168-175 it is argued: "'In Christ' clearly means those who believe in Christ.'" (p. 169). The "ambiguous half-sentence of the 1932 Brief Statement" ["Scripture teaches that God has already declared the whole world to be righteous in Christ, Rom. 5:19; 2 Cor. 5:18-21; Rom. 4:25"] is then re-interpreted accordingly (p. 175). Indeed: "A more precise definition (of those who are 'in Christ') is God's elect, since God already knows who the believers are ... He also knows which current 'believers' will fall permanently away..." (p. 169, note 359). All this is quite impossible, as has been amply shown above. In the context of objective justification "in Christ" means exactly what it means in II Cor. 5:19: "God was IN CHRIST reconciling the world to Himself." It was done for the whole world, not only for believers, or even only the elect — although only believers actually receive the benefit. It can easily be shown that by God regarding the world "'in Christ" or "outside of Christ" the 1872 Synodical Conference essay meant not the difference between believers and unbelievers, as HD. p. 169, fancies, but the difference between Law and Gospel, both of them being addressed to all mankind! "The law always accuses us and thus always shows us an angry God," says the *Apology* (IV, 295). In the law we all, believers and unbelievers, confront the wrath of God — and the Gospel of His grace and mercy is intended for and offered to all, but only believers accept and receive it.

The 1991 Missouri Synod Catechism

As a member of the task force charged with revising the 1943 explanation of the *Small Catechism* I can honestly say that apart from the specific Synodical directions to take notice of current issues (evolution, abortion, historical criticism), our one intention was to be faithful to Luther's original, also to its popularity and simplicity. The *Large Catechism* was allowed to interpret the *Small Catechism,* and citations from the Book of Concord were deliberately added where appropriate. There was never any question of changing the theology. This is not to say that the wording chosen was always the best or is beyond criticism. The criticism in *HD,* pp. 75-94, however is neither fair nor factual:

• Much is made (pp. 76-79) of the change from "redeemed" to "rescued" in respect of death and the devil (Q. 136 and 137). Now, in the original German Catechism the same word [erloeset] is used both in the meaning of the Second Article, and in the answer to the question. What does Baptism give or profit? In the latter case we are quite used to the English version, "delivers from death and the devil." The word "rescue" is simply the best contemporary and vivid equivalent of "deliver." It also reflects the Latin verb liberare, liberate, used in both places indicated. Far from "push[ing]" the "work of the Holy Ghost and the means of grace ... into the background" (p. 77), the new Catechism has considerably strengthened the stress on the means of grace (see for instance the new Questions 164, 236, 237, 238, 252).

• The new Catechism is criticized (p. 78) for suggesting "a benefit to us solely from the Redemption," by its Q. 139: "How does this work of redemption benefit you?" Neither the question nor the answer however, in any way suggests that the Holy Spirit, the means of grace, and faith may be dispensed with. In its "central" (9") thesis, on the means of grace, Walther's Gesetz und Evangelium (1897) cites Luther: "So this then is the benefit [Nutz] of the suffering and Resurrection of Christ, that He has done this not for Himself, but for the whole world that he has trodden underfoot the devil and my sin, which hung upon Him on Good Friday, so that the devil also flees before the Name of Christ. If now you want to make use of these great benefits [Gueter]: very well. He has already made a gift of them to you" (p. 164).

• The change from "willing to work all this in every one who hears the Gospel" to "want to do this in the lives of all people" (Q. 167, HD, p. 82) merely simplifies the language and incorporates the truth that the Gospel is intended for all humanity. HD wrongly uses the doctrine of election to limit the universality of the Gospel.

• I concede (HD, pp. 83 ff.) that the new Questions 180 and 182 on forgiveness are formulated somewhat unguardedly. In retrospect, I prefer the 1943 wordings. However, the following questions make it quite clear that forgiveness is given only in the Gospel and received only through faith. HD, p. 87, appeals to "the key word promise" in an earlier Catechism, but the new Q. 185 stresses the same "key word." Unlike a misconstrued ("Kokomo") version of objective justification, which indeed "undermines the concept of promise" (p. 87), the 1991 Cate-

chism, by its stress on the Gospel and Sacraments, uplifts and cele-
brates the divine promises in Christ.

6. Conclusion

If it is granted, on the one hand, that "No Orthodox Lutheran disputes
the fact that Christ's vicarious satisfaction reconciled God *toward* all
men, since that is the clear language of Scripture itself," that "the forgiveness of sins is 'universal,' as long as that is understood to mean only
that Christ's vicarious satisfaction *procured* this forgiveness for all
mankind" (*HD*. pp. 123, 234), and that objective justification may rightly
be understood as the assertion of *grace alone* against Rome, of *universal
grace* against Geneva, and of the *means of grace* against both (p. 39); and
if, on the other hand, it is granted that the "Kokomo" version of objective
justification is an aberration, and that the proper distinction of Law and
Gospel requires the teaching both of the wrath of God and of the pivotal
indispensable role of the means of grace, then a great deal of common
ground exists for pursuing a genuine meeting of the minds.

In these interests I have attempted, to the best of my ability, to sort
out the issues without rancor. It is difficult for us humans to put aside
pain and bitterness, but the Lord never ceases to invite us to this grace
or "following in His steps" (I Pet. 2:21). May He bless all who love His
saving truth, with mutual forbearance, humility, and charity. That is my
earnest plea and prayer. "Behold how good and pleasant it is for brethren
to dwell together in unity" (Ps. 133)!

Epiphany II, 1998 +++++++++++++ Respectfully submitted,
K. Marquart, C.T.S., Ft. Wayne, IN

Christian News, February 9, 1998

Endnotes

1 I shalt be referring to two works by Mr. Darby: *The Historical Development of "Objective Justification"* (published by the author, no date); and *Objective Justification*, correspondence with the Rev. Rolf Preus. Published in late 1997. I shall abbreviate the first as
HD and the second as *OJ*.

2 Henry P. Hamann, *Justification by Faith in Modern Theology*, Graduate Study No. 2
(St. Louis: School for Graduate Studies, Concordia Seminary, 1957), p. 60.

3 L. Berkhof, *Systematic Theology* (Grand Rapids: Eerdmans, 1974), p. 517.

4 I have covered this ground in "The Reformation Roots of 'Objective Justification,'" in
K. Marquart, J. Stephenson, B. Teigen, eds., *A Lively Legacy: Essays in Honor of Robert
Preus* [Ft. Wayne: Concordia Theological Seminary, 1985], pp. 117-130. The quotations are,
respectively, from Abraham Calov, *Exegema Augustanae Confessionis* (Wittenberg, 1665),
p. 4, and from John Benedict Carpzov, *Isagoge in Libros Ecclesiarum Lutheranarum Sym-
bolicos* (Leipzig, 1675), pp. 208 ff., cited in Walther-Baier, *Compendium Theologiae Positivae* (St. Louis: Concordia, 1879). vol. III, p. 285.

5 Hans Kueng, *Justification*. Philadelphia: Westminster, 1981. The original German
work appeared in 1957.

6 *HD*, p. 226.

7 "Justification and Easter: A Study in Subjective and Objective Justification in
Lutheran Theology," pp. 52-78.

8 A. Hoenecke, *Evangelisch-Lutherische Dogmatik* (Milwaukee: Northwestern, 1912),
vol. III, p. 191.

9 Jeffrey J. Kloha and Ronald R. Feuerhahn, eds., *Scripture and the Church: Selected
Essays of Hermann Sasse*. Concordia Seminary Monograph Series No. 2 (St. Louis: Concordia Seminary, 1995), p. 205.

10 The quote appears on the first page of George Stoeckhardt, "General Justification," translated by Otto F. Stahlke, *Concordia Theological Quarterly,* vol. 42, no. 2 (April 1978), pp. 139-144.

11 F. Pieper, "The Synodical Conference," in The Distinctive Doctrines and Usages of the General Bodies of the Evangelical Lutheran Church in the United States, 3rd ed. (Philadelphia The Lutheran Publication Society, 1893 and 1902), p. 148.

12 The words quoted immediately follow upon these crisp definitions: "Justification is an action of God, which occurs in time and with every single sinner individually. But there is also a universal justification, which happened (ergangen) in time upon all men, namely in Christ's passion and Resurrection" (my translation).

1. Biblically, justification is ____ act, which faith receives or ____, but does not ____.
2. Faith does not create forgiveness but only ____.
3. Forgiveness of sins is the same as ____.
4. Without ____ no one benefits one whit.
5. Are the inmates of Hell granted the status of saints? ____
6. Marquart recognized that in his effort to shield Siegbert Becker in the "Kokomo" affair ___ was right and ____ was wrong.
7. When it comes to redemption what defines the irreversible order? ___
8. Pieper wrote that a change of heart took place not in ___ but in ____.
9. The great Wisconsin Synod dogmatician A. Hoenecke used more careful language when he ____.
10. Outside of Christ God remains ____.
11. Did Marquart agree with all of Hermann Sasse's criticism of Missouri Synod theology? ____
12. What did Sasse write about the Missouri Synod and the Lutheran Confessions? ____
13. What did Schleiermacher teach? ____
14. According to Larry Darby, there is no ____.
15. Justification is by definition a ____ act.
16. The Resurrection of Christ involves ____ of the whole world.
17. What do the Jehovah's' Witnesses maintain fraudulently? ____
18. The New Testament economy of salvation culminates in the ____.
19. Does the Lutheran Book of Concord specify how many books are in the Bible? ____
20. Whatever is not biblical is not ____.
21. Calvinism denies that Christ has died for ____.
22. What is the meaning of "*monstrum incertitudis?*" ____
23. Forgiveness always equals____.
24. The dear God has gifted us all with what Christ has won for us, but only he who has come to faith ____.
25. Are there any material or doctrinal changes made in the translation of Pieper's dogmatics from German to English? ____
26. Are there any differences between Pieper and Stoeckhardt on universal or objective justification? ____
27. The proper distinction of Law and Gospel requires the teaching of both ____ and ____.

INDEX

107